ARMING
AN UNARMED
POLICE:

POLICY AND PRACTICE
IN THE METROPOLITAN POLICE

P A J WADDINGTON

Series Editor:
MOLLIE WEATHERITT

The Police Foundation

Reports in the Police Foundation series are published as an information service. The analysis, arguments, conclusions and recommendations in this report are those of the authors and not necessarily those of the Foundation.

Police Foundation books are available from all good bookshops with distribution by Pinter Publishers, c/o Marston Book Services, PO Box 87, Oxford, OX1 4LB.

In case of difficulty or for mail orders, contact PSI/Police Foundation Books Distribution, 100 Park Village East, London, NW1 3SR, (Tel 01-387 2171)

British Library Cataloguing in Publication Data

Waddington, P.A.J. (Peter A.J.)
   Arming an unarmed police: policy and practice in the
   Metropolitan Police.
   1. London. Police. Metropolitan Police.
   Equipment. Firearms. Use
   I. Title
   363.2'3

ISBN 0-947692-09-6

Published by the Police Foundation
314/316 Vauxhall Bridge Road, London SW1V 1AA.
Printed by J E C Potter & Son Ltd, Stamford, Lincs.

CONTENTS

FOREWORD

I very much welcome this excellent, thought-provoking
publication, which identifies some of the many current
dilemmas of policing, as we try and adapt to the challenges of
our changing environment.

The level of reported crimes of violence in society today, and
in particular the increasing incidence of the use of firearms
in crime, give us all cause for much concern. How we, the
police, react to this changing situation will influence not
only future trends in armed crime, but also future public
perceptions of policing, and through this the very nature of
the relationship between police and the public.

The Metropolitan Police were pleased to offer Dr Waddington an
open door to examine our firearms training and equipment, and
to comment on our policy and operations. His careful and
detailed study has enabled him to set out clearly many of the
dilemmas involved in 'arming an unarmed police', and the hard
choices that regularly have to be made in trying to retain our
essential tradition of policing by consent, while fulfilling
our equal responsibility to society to apprehend the
perpetrators of armed crime and to protect the public from the
armed criminal.

Within this broad dilemma, there are many other difficult
decisions to be made. For example in the context of our
firearms policy, do we opt for the open carrying of weapons
with the consequent loss of our unarmed image, or do we choose
the concealed carrying of firearms, which may be publicly more
acceptable, but operationally less efficient; in the context
of training, do we train more officers to enhance our ability
to respond quickly, which means, given the limited resources
we have, the inevitable dilution of skills, or do we train
fewer officers so that those entrusted with lethal weapons are

better trained but perhaps not so readily available when the need arises?

None of these dilemmas is easily resolved, and Dr Waddington with typical frankness and honesty, recognises this in his book. As well as setting out the sometimes irreconcilable conflicts we face almost daily, he provides a comprehensive account of our firearms training and equipment, and our policy on firearms use in the Metropolitan Police.

This publication makes a number of interesting recommendations which we shall, of course, consider. It will certainly help to inform the important debate on firearms and policing, and in doing so, will help us all ensure that the best decisions are ultimately made.

I am determined that there will be no escalation in the arming of London's police. However I am equally determined to provide the citizens of London with the protection from the terrorist and armed criminal, which regrettably today they very much need. This report will help all those involved in making those difficult decisions to achieve that subtle balance between what is practically essential and what is philosophically ideal.

Peter Imbert   1988

ACKNOWLEDGEMENTS

This report is part of a continuing research project, commissioned by the Police Foundation, into police use of force. It addresses one of the most controversial and sensitive issues in modern policing – the use of potentially lethal force by what we have been proud to traditionally describe as our *unarmed* police. The research has only been made possible by the fullest cooperation received from all ranks of the Metropolitan Police. I am, therefore, indebted to Sir Kenneth Newman, the Commissioner of the Metropolitan Police at the time the research commenced, and to Peter Imbert, who was then Deputy Commissioner and has now succeeded Sir Kenneth, both of whom supported and encouraged the research from the beginning. Their willingness to allow complete access to hitherto confidential internal documentation, to interview serving police officers and to permit my participation in training courses for armed officers is ample testimony to their justified confidence in the Metropolitan Police.

I am particularly grateful to all members of the Force Firearms Unit, formerly known as D11 and now, following reorganisation, known as PT17. All members of the Unit welcomed me and tolerated my inquiries with good humour and friendliness. My thanks go especially to Chief Superintendent Bob Wells for his courtesy and frankness. Also to Inspector, now Chief Inspector, Mike Waldren for taking the time to educate me in some of the technicalities of firearms and firearms tactics, and correcting an earlier draft of this report. To Sergeants Ian Matheson, Russ Parkin and Tony Windsor, and PCs Tom Tanner and Nigel Lloyd for treating me as just another trainee AFO. To the members of the Basic Firearms Course who accepted me as one of them despite the fact that I would never have to face the dangers and dilemmas that they might face. To members of the first 'Level II' training course for their hospitality and consideration. To all those instructors and officers on the various refresher courses who tolerated with extremely good grace my presence. Finally, to all those, too numerous to mention, who treated me with kindness and consideration.

Writing this report has been a labour I have shared with others. I have already expressed my thanks to Mike Waldren for the technical assistance he gave me. My thanks also go to Professor Tony Smith and Peter Schofield, both of the Department of Law, University of Reading, and to Mollie Weatheritt, Deputy Director of the Police Foundation, for taking the time to read and help me translate my thoughts into English. I am particularly indebted to Peter Schofield who, as a pacifist, read this account of guns and shootings with repugnance, but was the more able, thereby, to challenge any ill-thought-out arguments. My thanks also go to Chris Leslie and Hilary Vines, of the University of Reading Computer Centre, for their assistance in transforming the text into camera ready copy. Finally, my thanks to Barrie Irving and the Police Foundation for commissioning and publishing this report.

P.A.J. Waddington   1987

CHAPTER ONE

INTRODUCTION

The Dilemma of Arming an Unarmed Police

The central dilemma facing the British police is that on the one hand they are a coercive force (Bittner 1970, 1974) empowered to use violence, but, on the other, the legitimacy of police authority has been founded upon the benign, non-aggressive image of the unarmed British bobby (Reiner 1985, Miller 1977, Stead 1985). Thus, whilst it is ultimately the role of the police to use force to secure compliance, the overt use of force, especially resort to lethal force, damages their benign non-aggressive image. It is noticeable how, following even the most obviously justified shooting by police, official and semi-official spokesmen are asked or feel it necessary to *defend* or *justify* police action. For example, following the twin incidents in November 1987, when Avon and Somerset Police shot a man wielding a shotgun after he had been trapped in a narrow country lane following a long chase, followed a day later by Metropolitan Police shooting dead one of a gang of armed robbers during an exchange of fire after the robbers had been cornered, the Parliamentary spokesman for the Police Federation felt it necessary to reject any suggestion that the police were 'trigger-happy' and the Home Secretary was described as 'defending' police action.

Whilst any citizen can legally use 'reasonable force' in self-defence, the prevention of crime, and the arrest of offenders and persons unlawfully at large (Criminal Law Act 1967, s. 3), it is the police who have become specialists in the use of legitimate violence. Thus, the law expects the ordinary citizen to retreat from a threat before using force in self-

- 1 -

defence, whereas it is the duty of the police to enter threatening situations in anticipation of using force. People other than the police may be legally entitled to use force in specific conditions, but tend, nevertheless, to leave the exercise of coercion to the police. For example, police may accompany social workers to apprehend psychiatric patients in need of compulsory treatment and also bailiffs in the process of evicting trespassers. It is the police who have the authority to use force and it is they who may ultimately be responsible for the use of lethal force. For example, it is virtually inconceivable that any other citizen could lawfully decide to shoot someone using a highpowered rifle with a telescopic sight as might a police officer acting as a sniper against an armed criminal or terrorist.

The problem that the existence of such a coercive force creates is that ordinary citizens might feel oppressed by it. There was a long struggle to introduce a professional police in Britain prior to 1829. It was feared that a police force would itself threaten liberty (Critchley, 1970, 1978; Emsley, 1983; Stead, 1985). As Berki (1986) has recently noted there remains an ambivalence towards state authority. On the one hand, it secures one's freedom by preventing others from interfering with one's liberty, but, on the other, it limits that same freedom in order to provide security for others.

The British police, almost uniquely, succeeded in overcoming the initial hostility with which they were received and achieved widespread public acceptance by presenting an image of vulnerability, instead of the invincibility of their Continental (Emsley 1983, Stead 1985) or American (Miller 1977) counterparts. Unlike the police of most other countries, they did not, and still do not, seek to present the formidable appearance of the heavily armed officer. Indeed, it was the explicit intention of Sir Robert Peel that the 'bobbies' who were introduced on to the streets of London in 1829 should avoid giving the appearance of a military force, hence their uniform of top hat and frock coat. In contrast to virtually every other police force throughout the world, the British police officer does not carry a gun openly. He carries only a truncheon and even that is secreted in a trouser pocket. Indeed, the Metropolitan Police must be the only police force actually to disarm its officers, for the cutlasses, regularly issued to mounted officers and occasionally to foot patrols during the early years of the force, fell into increasing disuse and were eventually withdrawn.

Thus, unlike police officers in many other countries, the British police officer does not routinely secure compliance by his capacity to coerce, for he has limited ability to do so. Compliance is achieved, by and large, with the consent of the policed: citizens respect police authority. This ability to obtain compliance without coercion is what has long been considered the 'British police advantage'. Certainly accounts of policing in other countries often portray a much more adversarial and potentially violent relationship between the police and the public (Rubinstein 1973, Punch 1979).

However, the non-aggressive image of the British bobby has always been something of a myth. Not all of the public, all of the time, have been so compliant. On the contrary, the 150 years since the police were introduced on to the streets of London have often been unruly and occasionally tumultuous (Critchley 1970). Police have, as monopolists of force, been called upon to disperse rioters and arrest violently resisting criminals. This has involved them in the overt use of force. Indeed, the act of arresting someone is a use of force, albeit that it is often accomplished without recourse to actual violence. On these occasions the reality underlying the myth is manifested: the police *are* a coercive force. Never is this more obviously so than when the police resort to lethal force, for this challenges the fundamental element of the non-aggressive image - the fact that the British police, unlike others, are *unarmed*. The armed officer is no longer the vulnerable symbol of state authority, but the formidable symbol of coercive power.

In fact, the Metropolitan Police has never been an entirely unarmed force - firearms have always been available and in 1883 permission was granted for officers on the outer divisions to carry revolvers during night duty (Gould and Waldren 1986). However, the Metropolitan Police has historically adopted an explicit policy of minimising its preparedness for, and competence in, using firearms. Guns were

resorted to only occasionally and the police gave low priority
to training, relying instead upon the training some officers
had previously received during military service (Gould and
Waldren 1986, Hoare 1980).

> In the very rare cases where arms had to be used the
> British police showed an almost endearing incompetence
> and seemed quite proud of a total unfamiliarity with
> their weapons and sensible methods of dealing with such
> cases. (Greenwood 1979, p 1)

Thus, the benign impression was maintained: the public need
not have feared the police, because the police lacked the
competence to act as an oppressive force.

The apparent growth of armed crime and terrorism has changed
all that, for if armed criminals are to be captured and the
public protected from terrorists, it may be essential to arm
at least some of the police some of the time. The use of
firearms by the police has become increasingly evident in
recent years apparently in response to the increase in violent
crime and terrorism. It was estimated by Hoare (1980) that
some 3,000 officers in the Metropolitan Police (between 12 and
15 per cent of the force) were authorised to carry a firearm
on duty. It has become evident also that some officers are
virtually permanently armed, such as those engaged in
diplomatic, royalty and ministerial protection. Some officers
at Heathrow and other major international airports now carry
what appear to be sub-machine guns openly so as to deter an
attack by terrorists.

This growing use of firearms by the police has thrown into
sharp relief the central dilemma between the reality that
police are monopolists of force and their image of
vulnerability and non-aggression. As the use of firearms has
grown so too has public anxiety. A series of incidents
stretching back to the early 1970s has contributed to a sense
of public unease. In 1972 an officer on diplomatic protection
duty exchanged shots with bank robbers whom he surprised,
leaving one bank robber dead, another wounded and the officer
seriously injured. A few weeks later officers from the Special
Patrol Group responded to a reported hostage-taking at the

Indian Embassy and shot and killed two of the youthful would-be hostage-takers who were later found to have been armed with replica weapons (Gould and Waldren 1986). More recently, in 1982, police shot and seriously wounded Stephen Waldorf whom they had mistaken for the dangerous escaped prisoner, David Martin. In 1905 Mrs. Cherry Groce was also mistakenly shot and seriously wounded during an early morning raid on her house by officers searching for her son. Elsewhere, in 1983 officers in the West Midlands exchanged fire with a man on a darkened landing who was using his girlfriend as a shield, killing her by mistake. In 1985 a West Midlands officer, PC Chester, accidentally discharged his gun during an early morning raid and killed a five year old boy, John Shorthouse. Each of these events occasioned public alarm and concern about the selection, training and supervision of armed officers and the policy governing the use of police firearms.

Public apprehension was not now directed towards the fear of a force capable of oppressing the citizenry by armed might, but focused on the very incompetence that had hitherto been found so 'endearing' (Greenwood 1979). These events merely served to confirm Greenwood's prophetic remarks:

> In no field is the price of incompetence so high as in armed operations . . . No subsequent action, no recriminations and no compensation can bring to life the innocent citizen or the police officer needlessly killed. Nothing will destroy confidence in the police more thoroughly than the apparently ill trained and ill disciplined policeman who kills or maims the innocent or who, through his incompetence, fails to protect the public from a dangerous offender. (Greenwood 1979, p 3)

From 'Amateurism' to 'Professionalism'

Recognition that the traditional 'low key' approach to police use of firearms was no longer appropriate began in 1966 following the murder of three unarmed detectives in Shepherds Bush. Following so shortly after the abolition of the death penalty for the murder of police officers, this incident might have appeared at the time to usher in a new era in which police would increasingly confront armed criminals who were prepared to kill in order to escape arrest. What seems fairly certain is that it did prompt a fundamental change in police thinking about their use of firearms.

> The amateur phase was about to end, and the safety of officers and the public would now depend on highly trained and disciplined men being able to act as a professional body . . . The police would no longer be able to pay lip service to gun training, police firearms would be public knowledge, and their effective use would involve tactics which were alien to the British Bobby image. (Hoare 1980, p 72)

The most immediate consequence of this change was the establishment of the Firearms Training Department (which was to become famous under its title 'D11' until that designation was abandoned in the force reorganisation of 1986 [Gould and Waldren 1986, ch 7]). The Home Office set up a Working Party on Firearms for Police Use in Peacetime which published an interim report in 1971 as a result of which the Home Office issued a circular recommending certain types of weapon. This was supported by a report from the Home Office Scientific Advisory Branch (Home Office 1972) giving details of the recommended weapons. However, it was not until 1979 that the Association of Chief Police Officers convened the Joint Standing Committee on Police Issue of Firearms to standardise training and procedures throughout the country. In 1983 this resulted in the publication of the ACPO Manual of Guidance which forms the basis of policy for the Metropolitan Police as it does for all other forces in Britain. Although officially secret, these manuals are very largely consistent with Colin Greenwood's, *Police Tactics in Armed Operations* (1979).

Thus, the period from 1966 has seen a progressive adoption of an explicitly professional approach towards the police use of firearms. The police no longer pretend that they do not use firearms. They now seek public acceptance by relying upon high standards of expertise and systematic training. For example, in stark contrast to the traditional policy of minimising the use of firearms, police firearms training was publicised by the Metropolitan Police when, in 1985, journalists were allowed to visit Lippitt's Hill and observe officers under training.

This report will consider how the police have responded to this transition from 'endearing incompetence' to armed professionalism. It is presented in two parts: the first is frankly expository and will describe how armed officers are organised and deployed, what weapons are used, and how officers are trained to use them. The second will consider the issues that arise from arming the police. Attention will focus on handguns, sub-machine guns, shotguns and rifles, and the equipment that is ancillary to their use. It will not be concerned with baton guns, designed to fire plastic baton rounds, for they will be dealt with in a later paper concerning public order policing.

Part One

The Formal Organisation

of Armed Police

CHAPTER TWO

FORMAL POLICY

Current Policy

The policy of the Metropolitan Police as stated in the official manual of guidance, which is consistent with that adopted by all other British police forces, is to take all reasonable steps to ensure that armed incidents are concluded peacefully. First priority is placed upon the safety of innocent members of the public, second the safety of police officers and, finally, the safety of the suspect. Thus, direct confrontation between police and armed suspects is to be avoided unless it is necessary for the safety of innocent parties, such as hostages, or to secure essential evidence, as in the case of drugs raids.

Thus, emphasis is given to the 'containment' of an armed person. This is achieved by establishing two cordons, an inner cordon, or 'cover group', of armed officers who may be needed to engage the armed person if he attempts to escape; and an outer cordon, or 'perimeter group', of usually unarmed officers who keep bystanders away from the scene. Officers arriving at the location do so by a pre-arranged route avoiding the need to pass within range of the armed person and report to a 'rendezvous point' again out of range of the armed person.

Once the situation has been contained, officers will normally seek to make contact with the person, most often by telephoning the address or by hailing him. They will then endeavour to arrange his peaceful surrender. Only if there is some immediate threat to life will officers enter the premises as a 'raid group'. However, if no contact is established and there is no sign of life for many hours, officers may enter and search the premises. This is a slow, quiet and painstaking process whereby a team of officers enter the building and with each covering the other, search every room systematically. 'Forced entry' is the method of last resort usually justified to rescue hostages in immediate danger or to secure easily destroyed evidence such as drugs. Except in the most unusual circumstances it is left to specialist officers of the tactical firearms unit formerly known as D11. This unit contains 57 officers who spend most of their time as firearms instructors, but can be deployed in an operational role if the situation demands their expertise.

This approach was conspicuously seen in operation during several major sieges during the 1970s and early 1980s. At the 'Spaghetti House' Restaurant a gang of armed robbers took several members of the staff hostage for four days during September 1975 whilst police patiently awaited their surrender. Also in 1975 four IRA terrorists were trapped and took a middle-aged couple hostage in their Balcombe Street council flat where they remained for six days before their eventual surrender on the 12th December. Less successful in securing a peaceful outcome was the Iranian Embassy siege of 1980, which after several days of patient negotiation was ended by the SAS assault after the terrorists had begun killing their hostages. Despite some newspaper speculation to the contrary at the time, this did not lead to any abandonment of the 'softly softly' policy. Since that siege there have been several sieges involving criminals which have not resulted in bloodshed. The police must retain the option of mounting an assault if hostages are at risk, as they did during a siege at Northolt during the Christmas of 1985 when Errol Walker was shot during an operation to release his four year old hostage. However, just as at the Spaghetti House and Balcombe Street sieges, the policy continues to be that of containment designed to achieve a peaceful outcome.

In sum, the policy of the Metropolitan Police, reflecting that of the Home Office and the advice of the Association of Chief Police Officers is one of systematic caution.

The Organisation of Armed Police

Since the review which accompanied the Report of the Home Office Working Party (1986a), armed police in London have been organised into a three-tiered hierarchy.

The basic and broadest tier consists of 'Authorised Firearms Officers', or AFOs as they are widely known. They are the officers who are most commonly authorised to carry a gun and provide the initial response to most armed incidents. The AFO will normally be a uniformed patrol officer working on division and will be unarmed for the vast majority of the time. In the event of an armed incident, for example a suspected armed hostage-taking, this officer will receive authorisation to draw a firearm by a senior officer of Commander rank (or his deputy) and be deployed to the scene. The gun will be obtained from a station at which weapons are held and he will only be allowed to draw the weapon for which he is currently authorised (that is, the weapon he has been trained to use and in the use of which he has been reclassified as proficient within the past three months). When the incident is over he will return the gun to the station from which it came and continue with his routine police work.

In the past, these officers have also provided armed support during various types of raids, where there was reason to believe that police might encounter armed criminals. It was also the case, until the Home Office Working Party Report (1986a), which followed the shooting of Mrs. Groce, that some CID officers would also be AFOs, but this has been discontinued. Some plain clothes officers still remain AFOs, principally detectives working on 'central squads', such as the Robbery Squad and Anti-Terrorist Squad, who, because of the nature of their work, are likely to encounter armed criminals. Various other specialist squads and departments also contain AFOs; sometimes being an AFO is a requirement for membership of such a squad. Perhaps the largest of these is the Royalty and Diplomatic Protection Department, whose members provide both uniformed protection of sensitive locations and plain clothes bodyguards to high-risk royalty, diplomats and ministers of the Crown. The Special Escort Group, who provide escorts for high-risk persons, such as state dignitaries, terrorist prisoners and high risk consignments are also usually AFOs.

A recent addition to the organisational structure has been to further strengthen the role of the Force Firearms Unit, now known by the designation 'PT17', but made famous as 'D11'. This Unit has always provided firearms instructors to act in an operational capacity when the situation demanded their specialist expertise. These instructors retain this role, but in addition another strata of expertise has been introduced in the guise of 'Level II' officers. These consist of three groups of six constables and a sergeant who are based at the headquarters of the Force Firearms Unit and respond to incidents which demand greater expertise than that possessed by AFOs. 'Level II' officers are more highly trained, practise regularly and work as a team in a way that officers committed to other duties find impossible. It is intended that they should take over the entry into premises and the surrender of armed suspects. Henceforth, it is intended that AFOs will provide the initial response and constitute the 'cover group', but 'Level II' officers will then attend to take over more serious incidents. 'Level II' will also take over the task of providing armed support for raids on premises. In addition to the uniformed 'Level II' teams, it is also intended that the plain clothes central squads will have available two teams of officers trained to the 'Level II' standard.

Firearms instructors now constitute the 'Level I' teams who deal with incidents which exceed the expertise of and equipment available to 'Level II' officers. These instructors spend one week in six training together as a team and a further week on operational duties. They are considered to be very much the elite. For example, it is they who, save in the most exceptional circumstances, would effect an 'forced entry' to rescue hostages.

Aside from this hierarchy, there are 'force riflemen' who, like AFOs, undertake unarmed patrol duties for the majority of their time. However, if an incident or event occurs where it is thought necessary to provide long-range cover by the use of rifles with telescopic sights, then it is these officers who are called upon. It was they who featured prominently in the

BBC TV documentary 'The Queen's Peace' (*Police* 1986). Another group which falls outside the three-level hierarchy is the 'Security Section' at Heathrow Airport. Apart from being qualified to carry the standard revolver, many of these officers are also authorised to carry the Browning self-loading pistol and the Heckler and Koch MP5 carbine. Because of the sensitive nature of their duties and the responsibility it entails, they have to satisfy rather more demanding standards and complete refresher training and 'authorisation' tests once per month. Consistent with general policy, the aim is to raise standards and make training increasingly realistic. For example, instead of standing in a static position at the end of the range, officers are instructed to move around and engage the target from whatever position they happen to be in when it comes into view.

In January 1987 an incident occurred which highlighted another form of armed deployment. Two men were pursued south along the M1 by officers from the Nottinghamshire Constabulary. When they were eventually halted between junctions 12 and 13 in Northamptonshire they fired at the police who had stopped them. However, the police were quickly able to return fire because theirs was an 'armed response vehicle' in which firearms were routinely carried and available for use on the authority of an Assistant Chief Constable. The public discussion that this incident prompted revealed that Nottinghamshire were not alone in deploying such vehicles. The Home Office Working Group received evidence that two forces had such a policy (Home Office, 1986a). The Metropolitan Police acknowledged that they too had an armed response vehicle manned by members of the Royalty and Diplomatic Protection Department, whose officers protect sensitive locations such as embassies, and people at risk of assassination or attack, such as Ministers of the Crown.

In fact, there is nothing new in this kind of deployment, especially in London (Roberts 1973). It was officers from such a vehicle, then the responsibility of the Special Patrol Group, who responded to the hostage-taking at India House in 1972, where they entered and shot dead two youths. In 1977 this responsibility was transferred from the SPG to the Diplomatic Protection Group (as it was then known) and assigned to a vehicle with the call sign 'Ranger 500'. Although dedicated to diplomatic protection – it was one of the first vehicles to respond to the shooting outside the Libyan Peoples' Bureau in which WPC Yvonne Fletcher was killed in April 1984 – the officers who man this vehicle are still police officers and can be deployed to armed incidents occurring within the Central London area (see reply to Mr. Blom-Cooper, Home Office 1986a). It should be remembered that PC Peter Sliman was a DPG officer en route to an embassy in January 1972 when he encountered armed robbers, one of whom he shot dead.

Conclusion

Official policy and formal organisation have developed over recent years in response to the need for more frequent armed operations. The official policy (see Greenwood 1979) emphasises safety and caution. The aim is not to 'shoot it out' with a suspected gunman, but to contain him and persuade him to surrender. The officers who are responsible for implementing this policy have become fewer and more highly specialised. They are now organised into a hierarchical structure in which AFOs are normally expected only to provide the initial response and containment. More demanding tasks are intended to be reserved for full-time armed officers of either 'Level I' or 'Level II' standard.

CHAPTER THREE

WEAPONRY

Revolvers

The basic weapon which AFOs are authorised to carry is the revolver. This is a readily concealed, easy to use and versatile weapon for use at close range, which is appropriate for the majority of occasions when a firearm is needed. The Home Office guidelines state that the revolver should be capable of firing .38" special + P ammunition which is of the 'semi-wadcutter, semi-jacketed' variety (that is, the bullet's nose is flattened, rather than dome-shaped, and only partially enclosed in a hard metal sheath designed to retain its integrity once it strikes the person's body). Individual forces are left free to decide which makes of weapon and ammunition to purchase. The Metropolitan Police, in company with most other forces, have adopted the Smith and Wesson model 10 as their standard issue firearm. This revolver has a four inch heavy barrel and holds six rounds in the cylinder. Metropolitan Police officers engaged in regular plain clothes duties are issued with the Smith and Wesson model 64, which is a stainless steel variant of the model 10 with a two inch barrel.

In the majority of instances, these guns are held in locked safes at police stations and issued to officers as and when necessary. Obviously, officers who carry a firearm regularly, for example, on protection duty, will normally be issued with the same weapon each time they report for work However, only firearms instructors and very few other specialist squads are issued with a revolver that they and they alone use. To take advantage of the fact that revolvers issued to instructors are 'personal issue' and, therefore, are not used by a variety of handlers, the weapons themselves are slightly more sophisticated, either the Smith and Wesson model 19 or model 28, each of which have sights that can be adjusted to the particular needs of the individual officer. These two weapons are also notable for the fact that they are capable of firing the .357" Magnum round (a very much more powerful cartridge than that issued to British police officers).

Self-loading Pistols

Apart from revolvers, the other type of handgun is the self-loading pistol, sometimes misleadingly described as an 'automatic' or 'semi-automatic' pistol. This is misleading, because whereas an 'automatic' weapon of any kind continues to fire repeatedly whilst the trigger is depressed, a self-loading weapon fires just one shot with each depression of the trigger. The confusion arises from the fact that self-loading and automatic weapons are both magazine fed, that is, the rounds are held in a magazine attached to the weapon and fed into the breech mechanism one at a time.

In recent years the Metropolitan Police have used two makes of self-loading pistol, the Walther PP 9mm and the Browning Hi-Power 9mm. The Walther was discontinued after the attempted assassination of Princess Anne when the gun carried by her protection officer jammed. The Metropolitan Police had carried a small stock of Brownings since the mid-1960s to arm officers escorting extremely high-value loads and in the mid-1970s the decision was taken also to arm officers of the Force Firearms Unit with this weapon in response to the growth of terrorist activity. It was felt that whereas armed encounters with criminals tended to involve a limited exchange of fire, that between terrorists and police might entail a prolonged exchange. The Browning carries up to thirteen rounds in its magazine (hence the manufacturer's description 'Hi-Power'), as compared to the seven rounds carried by the Walther, and six rounds carried by the model 10 revolver; it therefore offers greater firepower. It fires 9mm parabellum ammunition of either standard military 108 grain fully-jacketed round-nosed design or 95 grain semi-wadcutter semi-jacketed design.

Self-loading pistols operate in the following way: rounds are
stacked in a magazine under tension from a spring at the
magazine's base. When a round is fired, the recoil is used to
force the slide back, which causes the spent cartridge case to
be ejected and pushes the hammer into the single-action
position. As the slide returns to its initial position under
the pressure of a spring, the round located at the top of the
magazine is pushed up a ramp and into the breech ready to
fire. Despite its evident complexity, this mechanism is
operated with great speed and allows this type of weapon to be
fired very rapidly - as fast as the trigger can be depressed.

Holsters

Except for officers at Heathrow Airport who carry the Heckler
and Koch MP5 carbine overtly and are allowed also to display
their handgun, all handguns issued to Metropolitan Police
officers are carried covertly on the hip. Shoulder holsters
are rarely used because when drawing a gun from this type of
holster the gun is initially pointing to the rear, away from
the target (and therefore contrary to one of the safety
rules), and as the gun is then swung in an arc towards the
target this has the disadvantage that either a premature or
late shot will be fired at or about torso height missing the
target but endangering others. It is, in fact, difficult to
swing a gun laterally onto a target for two reasons: first the
width of the torso is less than its height so that if the gun
remains in motion there is less opportunity to hit the target.
Second, swinging the gun imparts lateral momentum which is
difficult to arrest once the gun is pointing at the target.

Thus, police officers almost universally use a hip holster, so
that when drawing and aiming their gun, it is always pointing
either at the floor in front of the person aimed at or in his
direction. If the person is missed, the shot will either
strike the floor or fly over the person's head, rather than be
fired at torso height (Greenwood 1966). This is obviously less
dangerous to innocent bystanders. It is also more difficult to

- 19 -

overswing the gun when moving through a vertical as opposed to
horizontal arc. Moreover, since the torso is longer than its
width, there is a greater likelihood that the shot fired will
actually hit the person, if not the torso.

Like the guns that are used, holsters are officially issued
and officers are not permitted to use any other. The basic
holster does not have a flap covering the butt of the gun,
which remains open and is secured by a 'thumb-break' strap.
When the butt is held the thumb pushes against a press-stud
which springs open allowing the gun to be drawn rapidly.
Officers at Heathrow who carry the Browning self-loading
pistol have a specially designed holster the strap of which
stretches across the rear of the slide forming a barrier
between the hammer and the firing pin. As the gun is held
prior to drawing it, the strap is pushed forward by the thumb
as it grips the butt. For those occasions where it is
essential that guns should be carried as covertly as possible,
there is a 'pancake' holster which is moulded to the curvature
of the body and thus minimises the bulge beneath clothing.
Officers who must carry a gun whilst in shirt sleeves are
issued with a holster that fits inside the trouser pocket,
into which the gun is then placed.

One problem that has arisen with the existing standard holster
is that the trigger guard is left uncovered, allowing an
officer to grasp not only the butt of the gun but also to
place his finger on the trigger as he draws it. This is
dangerous, because in the excitement of an operational
incident (or even occasionally on the practice range) the
trigger may be squeezed prematurely as the gun is drawn,
injuring the user. Holsters are about to be modified so that
the trigger guard is covered, thus inhibiting too early
contact with the trigger.

Sub-machine guns and carbines

Perhaps the most controversial weapon now supplied to police
is the sub-machine gun. The Stirling MkIV 9mm L2A3 machine-gun
has been carried covertly on board vehicles at Gatwick airport

since the mid-1970s and permission was granted for sub-machine guns to be purchased for the use of the Force Firearms Unit in 1977. However, they came to public attention with the visit of President Reagan in 1984 when it was announced that twelve Heckler and Koch MP5K sub-machine guns were to be purchased for protection officers. Then in the wake of the terrorist attacks on Rome and Vienna airports in December 1985, it was decided to arm officers at Heathrow airport with an adapted version of the Heckler and Koch MP5. These weapons are only carried with the express permission of the Home Secretary, from whom authorisation must be obtained each time the Heckler and Koch MP5K is carried for protection purposes and is granted on a monthly basis to officers carrying the Heckler and Koch MP5 at Heathrow Airport.

The Heckler and Koch MP5 fires a 9 mm parabellum round, identical to that fired by the Browning self-loading pistol. Essentially, the mechanism by which it operates is the same as that of the Browning. However, there is a distinction between this and some other makes of weapon, in that the Heckler and Koch MP5 fires in a 'closed bolt' not the 'open bolt' mode. This means that when the Heckler and Koch MP5 is fired the recoil mechanism ejects the spent cartridge, opens the firing mechanism and places another round in the breech ready to fire. When the trigger is depressed the firing pin strikes the bullet and fires it. The open bolt mechanism does not place a round into the breech until the trigger is depressed whereupon the round is pushed into the breech and fired in a single movement. Instructors maintain that the open bolt mechanism causes the weapon to move slightly making it less accurate; a claim implicitly acknowledged by a major supplier of 'open bolt' sub-machine guns, Stirling, who have now developed a 'closed bolt' carbine (the Mk7 C4 and C8) which is more accurate than the standard sub-machine gun upon which it is based.

The Heckler and Koch MP5 is capable of automatic fire, but can also be fired in single shot mode (and the MP5K has the further option of three-round bursts). Indeed, the weapons carried at Heathrow airport are adapted so that they can *only* be fired in the single shot mode. The advantage of using this weapon in single shot mode is that it affords greater accuracy over longer distances than can be achieved with a revolver. Its shoulder stock and two-handed grip, together with its eight inch barrel means that it is accurate up to 100 metres, compared to a maximum effective range of 50 metres for handguns (itself considered hopelessly optimistic by many). Its magazine of thirty rounds, with a second magazine carried in a separate holster on the hip also offers considerable firepower in a sustained gunfight with terrorists.

It was in order to provide firepower that the Heckler and Koch MP5K (that is, the shorter version with the twin pistol grips and no shoulder stock) was purchased for use by protection officers. Like their colleagues at Heathrow they are trained mainly to fire the gun in single shot mode, but, unlike officers at Heathrow, retain the option of automatic fire. Unlike the officers at Heathrow they do not carry this weapon overtly. It is carried inside the jacket on a shoulder strap. If needed, the gun is held in both hands and pushed away from the body against the shoulder strap, thus giving it stability. The eighteen round magazine is supplemented by a thirty round back-up magazine.

It is sometimes thought that sub-machine guns are designed to spray bullets rather than fire them accurately. This is not so, but it is true that the mechanism of automatic fire causes the weapon to ride upwards. Hence sub-machine guns are intended to be fired in short bursts and can be set to fire just three rounds with each depression of the trigger. However, most instructors claim that automatic fire is rarely necessary, because it is possible to 'double tap' (that is, fire a pair of shots in rapid succession) very rapidly and with great precision. Used in this single-shot mode, the Heckler and Koch MP5 is not a sub-machine gun, but a carbine (that is, a short rifle). Perhaps the only use of automatic fire would be in conditions such as the SAS assault on the Iranian Embassy in 1980 when terrorists had begun to kill hostages and were themselves armed with automatic weapons.

It is important to distinguish the sub-machine gun or carbine from other automatic weapons such as the Kalashnikov AK47 assault rifle, preferred by many terrorists. In contrast to the sub-machine gun which fires 9mm rounds, the AK47 is capable of firing 7.62mm high velocity ammunition which has a far more devastating effect on impact and is capable of penetrating concrete walls and other such obstacles. The Heckler and Koch MP5 should, by contrast, be considered as an intermediate weapon between the handgun and the high-velocity rifle.

Shotguns

Another intermediate range weapon available to police is the shotgun. This weapon enables armed officers to engage armed suspects, if necessary, at greater range and with more firepower than does a handgun.

Shotguns are smooth-bore weapons, that is, the interior of the barrel is *not* rifled so as to impart twist to the bullet as it travels along the barrel. The shotgun cartridge comprises a propellant, wadding and the shot itself. The latter varies from 'birdshot', which consists of approximately 200 tiny lead pellets, through a series of progressively fewer but heavier pellets until one reaches 'rifled slug' - a single massive slug of lead which is rifled so that it spins and maintains accuracy after leaving the barrel.

In addition, shotguns can discharge various specialist projectiles, most important for the police being the 'ferret' CS gas cartridge. This is a sack of CS liquid which can penetrate a door or window before bursting and discharging its contents as an aerosol into the room beyond and is designed for use against barricaded and armed persons.

In the Metropolitan Police the Force Firearms Unit are responsible for the use of shotguns and currently favour the Remington Model 870 12 bore pump action with and without folding stock. The 'pump action' shotgun is a single barrelled weapon which is fed by a tubular magazine lying parallel to and beneath the barrel. Cartridges are fed into the breech by drawing the forward grip towards the rear of the gun. This opens the breech and ejects the spent cartridge case. When the grip is pushed forward a fresh cartridge is inserted into the breech and the weapon is ready to fire in single-action. For use against persons the police use the cartridge commonly referred to by its sporting designation as SG or 'small game'. This is a cartridge containing nine pellets each of which strikes the target with roughly the ballistic effect of a .30" bullet and which together provide immense stopping power. By contrast, rifled slug is used to dispose of crazed animals that have to be destroyed from a distance, such as bulls that escape en route to the abattoir.

It may be thought that the shotgun is an inappropriate weapon for police to use and there was initial resistance to its proposed introduction in the 1960s (Greenwood 1966). This view seems to rest upon the myth that the shotgun causes pellets to spread widely in flight, hitting an area much greater than the intended target. In fact, the SG cartridge gives a spread of shot of around eight to ten inches at 15 metres, most of which would strike a person's torso if aimed in that direction. At the same time, the fact that shot does spread and some individual pellets might miss the armed person may make this an inappropriate weapon for use in crowded areas such as airport departure lounges. However, a recent report from the Sussex Police (Edwards and Menzies, 1986) suggests that some continental forces are actively examining the feasibility of this weapon in precisely this context.

Rifles

For engaging targets at long distance the police are equipped with high velocity rifles. The Metropolitan Police use three types: the Enfield Enforcer 7.62mm bolt-action sniper rifle firing 147 grain bullet; the Heckler and Koch HK93 .223" and Ruger mini 14R .223" self-loading rifles, each of which fire a 55 grain bullet. All of these rifles are fitted with appropriate telescopic sights and image intensifiers for use at night. The Enforcer is simply a modernised version of the standard military .303" Lee Enfield rifle, used by Force Firearms Unit and riflemen at Heathrow for long range positions. The Ruger is issued to divisional riflemen and is more suitable to shorter range work of up to 100 metres. The

Heckler and Koch HK93 is issued to officers of the Force Firearms Unit instead of the Ruger. All three models fire fully-jacketed high velocity ball ammunition, about which more will be said shortly.

Special Weapons

All the above are standard police or military weapons, but there are other specialist weapons issued to police. First, there is CS gas which can be delivered by either a hand-thrown grenade or fired from a launcher. Two types of launcher are used, the purpose made Webley/Schermuly 1.5" gas gun or the 'Ferret' cartridge fired from a 12 bore shotgun. Second, the police sometimes need to use 'stun' or, more accurately, 'distraction' grenades against a besieged hostage-taker. These are grenades which when thrown eject one or more capsules of explosive charge that explode with a bright flash and deafening bang of around 170 Db, startling and disorienting the person in the room for the few seconds it might take for officers to effect a safe entry. A version of this device was seen in operation at a hostage-taking during the Christmas of 1985 at Northolt when officers from the Force Firearms Unit shot Errol Walker who was in the act of stabbing his four year old hostage. Third, in effecting an entry the police have had to rely upon such methods as sledgehammers, which obviously lack speed. Currently under evaluation is the 'Hatton' round which consists of a single slug of concentrated lead dust fired from a 12 bore shotgun at either the lock or hinges of a door. Upon impact the slug disintegrates, but imparts sufficient energy to the door to dislodge the lock or hinges thereby causing it to open. The danger is that a dislodged fitment may fly off and injure someone in the room, but since it is designed for use in 'forced entry' when someone's life is in danger this might be thought to be a small risk to run. Also under consideration is a form of hydraulic ram which locks against the door jamb and then demolishes the door. This was used successfully at Grendon Underwood psychiatric prison in 1986 when a barricaded prisoner holding another prisoner hostage began to attack the latter.

Other Equipment

Apart from weapons designed for use against armed criminals and terrorists, police also have available a variety of defensive equipment to safeguard themselves from attack. The most commonly available is body armour, which is somewhat misleadingly described occasionally as the 'bullet proof vest'. This is a garment of waistcoat design which can be worn underneath or over a jacket and is secured by velcron straps. It consists of 16 to 18 layers of the fabric Kevlar which was originally developed to provide the bracing for vehicle tyres. It will prevent penetration from .38" ammunition up to and including .375" magnum rounds and standard 9mm. However, .44" magnum rounds will penetrate albeit with much reduced energy. Kevlar body armour is not 'bullet proof' because it will not offer protection from armour-tipped or high velocity ball ammunition.

Body armour takes two forms: light and heavy weight. These do not differ in the number of layers of Kevlar nor the protection offered from penetration. The difference lies in the fact that whilst light weight body armour may prevent a bullet from penetrating, the person wearing it will sustain quite severe internal injuries from the impact of the bullet. This so-called 'trauma effect' can be minimised by the addition of a 'trauma pad' of soft fabric material which absorbs the impact energy of the bullet. The disadvantages of wearing heavy weight body armour are that it is less comfortable to wear, especially in warm weather, and it is bulky and cannot be worn covertly under other garments.

In addition to basic body armour other equipment can improve the protection offered to officers confronting armed criminals and terrorists. Kevlar blankets can provide easily transported and rapidly assembled screening. Steel or ceramic plates can be inserted into the front and back portions of the body armour 'waistcoat', which greatly improves the protection offered, even from high-velocity rounds. Not only can ceramic plates be inserted into body armour to enhance protection, they can also be used externally as a portable shield, or what is called the 'ballistic clipboard'. Ceramics also used to provide protection to the head in the form of helmet which can be worn by officers dealing with armed criminals or terrorists. Recently the Force Firearms Unit has acquired a number of glass-reinforced plastic shields which armed officers can carry and which were used operationally for the first time at the Plumstead Abattoir incident in July 1987 when members of the Force Firearms Unit intercepted four armed robbers who were holding up a security van, shooting three of them, two of whom died. Larger shields are also available on wheels, which are designed to offer protective cover when moving towards the location of armed persons, perhaps in order to recover an injured person.

Apart from armour that is worn, carried or pushed, the police are equipped with armoured Land Rovers. These appear to be ordinary Land Rovers but are constructed from armour-plated steel, thus affording protection for passengers from most types of ammunition. However, their weight significantly reduces their speed and general performance. Following the 1985 riot at the Broadwater Farm Estate in Tottenham, where firearms were used against police, the Metropolitan Police borrowed from the army a number of military-styled armoured personnel carriers (known as 'pigs') to provide mobile cover for armed officers engaging armed rioters. These have now been replaced by 24 custom-built armoured Land Rovers designed for the purpose.

Dogs

Another resource available to armed officers is specially trained police dogs who may be used to search premises or vehicles for an armed person and/or to attack such a person. The special training is necessary to ensure that the dog does not attack police officers holding guns. Also, because the dog handler himself is not normally armed and should not be exposed to danger unnecessarily, the dog must perform its assigned task 'unsighted'. This means that whereas normally a dog-handler will point directly at, say, the person whom the dog is to apprehend, in an armed operation the handler must instruct the dog without being able to see the suspect directly, for that would require him to be exposed.

Dogs are particularly useful, because not only can they search an area and bark in such a manner as to indicate the presence of an armed person, but they can be used as a sub-lethal weapon in their own right. Thus, it has sometimes occurred that an armed suspect has apparently surrendered, but failed to comply with police instruction, for example, refusing to stop when told or to lay down a weapon. This puts an armed officer in a quandary, for it would be difficult to justify opening fire on a person not presenting an immediate threat, but it would be dangerous to approach the person himself. In such a situation a dog could be sent to apprehend the suspect. This obviously exposes the dog to danger, but this is less than might at first appear, because a fast running dog heading directly towards a gunman presents a small rapidly moving target which is difficult to hit. For this reason, these dogs are known colloquially as 'furry Exocets'.

Conclusions

Undoubtedly, the Metropolitan Police's armoury now contains a more extensive range of weaponry than would have been imagined only a few years ago. The basic weapon remains the .38" revolver. Only a few specialised officers have access to the more exotic firearms. Whether this weaponry is necessary or represents a gratuitous extension of armed might by the Metropolitan Police is a question to which we will return in a later chapter.

CHAPTER FOUR

TRAINING

Perhaps the clearest indication in the change of official attitude towards police use of firearms 'from amateurism to professionalism' is to be seen in the development of training. Training in the use of firearms in the Metropolitan Police occurs at several levels. AFOs receive a basic course, followed by regular refresher training; protection officers complete a special 'bodyguards' course; force riflemen also receive special training in the use of their weapons; 'Level II' officers complete a three-week special course and train regularly; and 'Level I' officers complete a six-week course, after which they follow a cycle of instructing others, team training and operational readiness.

The Basic Firearms Course

Basic firearms training has been gradually extended since it was first introduced on a systematic basis in 1966. It now lasts two weeks, at the end of which trainees are given a written and practical test before acquiring their authorisation to carry a revolver. Roughly half the time is spent on the practice range, acquiring shooting and handling skills. The other half is spent in the classroom being taught aspects of law and procedure or engaged in various practical exercises. (See *International Law Enforcement* 1985a and b.)

On the range, trainees fire at a man-sized target portraying a man wearing sunglasses holding a gun at waist height which is pointed towards the officer. The torso is marked by an oval and shots inside this area score two points, compared to shots hitting the target outside the torso which score one point. The targets swivel on their axis from the edge facing the trainee to the full face of the target being presented. The duration of the exposure of the target is varied for different tests. All shots are fired from the 'isosceles' position, that is, the officer faces the target squarely holding the gun in both hands with the arms fully extended. This is in contrast to the so-called 'Weaver' stance, favoured by the Federal Bureau of Investigation, in which the officer adopts a stance similar to that of a boxer with one foot forward of the other. In this stance, the gun is held in both hands, but only the strong arm is fully extended, whilst the weak arm is bent exerting a backward pressure. The officer looks along the length of the extended arm as he may do along a rifle. There is considerable controversy between advocates of each approach regarding the advantages and disadvantages of these competing methods. However, the Metropolitan Police are currently committed to the 'isosceles' position and this is taught without equivocation.

Officers are taught the two basic methods of double-handed shooting - 'sense of direction' and aimed. 'Sense of direction' shooting is designed for responding to surprise encounters at close range. At seven metres the officer is taught to punch the gun directly towards the target, whilst continuing to look at the target with both eyes. The punching action locks the arms and the parallax effect of keeping both eyes focused on the target whilst bringing the gun into the field of view causes the shape of the gun to superimpose upon that of the target when it is in the correct position. The officer then momentarily pauses before firing a pair of shots towards the target as rapidly as possible. The aim is to hit the torso of the target with both shots. This skill is tested in two examined 'shoots' of ten rounds each: in the first the officer must fire three pairs of shots, reload and fire the remaining two pairs at a static target within 25 seconds; in the second he must fire a pair of shots at a turning target which is exposed for two seconds each time.

Aimed shooting occurs under circumstances when the officer has time to sight the gun, usually from a distance of at least 15 metres, and fire a single shot. Unlike 'sense of direction' the attention of the officer is focused on the sights of the gun as he attempts to obtain and maintain a good 'sight picture'. This mode of shooting is tested at 15 and 25 metres. At 15 metres the officer is presented with a target that turns and remains exposed for three seconds, during which time he must bring his gun into the aim, align the sights and fire at the torso. At 25 metres it is envisaged that the officer will be behind protective cover which can also be used to support the gun. In one test the officer must fire two rounds free standing, two rounds standing using the support of the barricade, two rounds kneeling, two rounds sitting and, finally, two rounds lying down. Until recently this included firing two rounds with the weak hand (for example, a right-handed officer would fire using his left hand). This was based on the view that this would allow an officer to keep more of his body behind protective cover if he was obliged to fire from the right-hand side. However, weak-hand shooting is usually of such a poor standard and officers tend not to adopt it operationally, so it has now been discontinued.

Also discontinued is the single-action mode of shooting. This involves first 'cocking' the weapon manually and then firing it with a light touch on the trigger, rather than squeezing the trigger so that the cylinder rotates and the hammer is pulled back. The difference is that single-action requires approximately three pounds pressure on the trigger compared to the 10-13 pounds needed for double-action. The advantage of single-action is that the reduced pressure and shorter travel of the trigger allows greater accuracy which reduces the tendency of the aim to stray as the trigger is squeezed in double-action. The danger is that a gun in single-action is much more easily discharged. It has been decided that henceforth officers will be merely familiarised with single-action, if only to demonstrate its dangers, but not required to show competence in its use and they are instructed not to use it operationally. Instead of the 'single-action shoot' officers now complete a 'walkdown shoot'. That is, starting at 25 metres, officers walk line abreast down the range towards the target. When the targets turn they must fire an aimed shot. When they reach 10 metres they stop and fire a pair of shots at each turning target.

All classification shoots during the basic course require only that officers begin from the 'drawn weapons position', that is, the gun is drawn from the holster and held at waist height pointing towards the target. From this position it is brought to the aim and fired. This rests on the assumption that officers are unlikely to be surprised and need to draw their weapon rapidly from the holster and fire it. The basic course does include instruction on how to draw from the holster, but it is not until the officer begins refresher training that he will need to show proficiency in this mode of shooting.

An officer is required to obtain a total score of 70 per cent to receive authorisation and in no individual test should he obtain less than 50 per cent. A score of 90 per cent earns the appellation of 'marksman'. However, authorisation does not depend solely upon how well a person can shoot, although minimal competence is the *sine qua non* for passing the course. Throughout the course instructors assess each trainee to determine whether they have the necessary aptitude for authorisation. It is in a variety of theoretical and practical exercises that this aptitude is gauged.

Away from the practice range students are taught the law and internal police regulations governing the use of firearms. They are reminded that section 3 of the Criminal Law Act 1967 states that:

> A person may use such force as is reasonable in the circumstances for the prevention of crime, in effecting or assisting in the arrest of offenders or persons unlawfully at large.

This licences the use of deadly force only in exceptional circumstances as outlined by the 'strict reminder' in the Home Office guidelines:

> A firearm is to be used only as a last resort. Other methods must have been tried and failed, or must - because of the circumstances - be unlikely to succeed if tried. For example, a firearm may be fired when it is apparent that the police cannot achieve the lawful purpose of preventing the loss, or further loss, of life, by any other means. If it is reasonable to do so, an oral warning is to be given before opening fire.

And officers are forcefully reminded by those guidelines that:

> The responsibility for use of a firearm rests with the individual officer and he is answerable to the courts, both criminal and civil.

Both the seriousness of the task and responsibility of the officer discharging his duty are repeatedly affirmed by instructors, who use anecdotal examples to reinforce the dilemmas that officers face.

Apart from the general law and regulations governing the use of firearms, trainees are also taught the procedures to be adopted in various situations. For example, they are taught that in dealing with armed persons in buildings or other premises, the procedure is first to contain the situation, plan further action, organise personnel and then activate the plan. In containing the situation, they are told that it is important to protect the public and other police officers by placing an outer cordon around the scene and preventing entry and taking steps to evacuate, if necessary. To protect officers attending the scene it is essential to establish a rendezvous point which avoids their passing the premises in question. A system of colour coding and notation is used so that officers at different locations around the premises can provide a coherent picture both of the building and the events occurring therein (such as movement or noise) to the operational commander using only radio communication. Planning not only involves the possibility of a sudden raid, but includes subterfuge and, most important of all, direct contact by the use of the telephone or shouted conversation.

If all this sounds only commonsense, the course includes video and slide presentations of actual events in which commonsense did not prevail An incident in Oldham in the early 1970s, filmed by a local television crew, provides a vivid illustration of how officers failed adequately to safeguard the public. Their attempts to overpower an intoxicated man wielding a 9mm pistol in a house were generally chaotic and often dangerous to themselves and everyone else involved.

Another incident in Leicester a couple of years later left a police officer and ambulanceman dead, and others seriously wounded when the police responded to a fatal shooting in a disorganised and uncoordinated fashion.

Also emphasised is the level of threat posed by firearms, especially shotguns. Slides of scenes where shotguns have been used and the mortuary photographs of victims demonstrate the lethality of this and other weapons. Trainees are taken onto the range where an instructor demonstrates how little protection is afforded against shotgun pellets by doors and similar barriers. A two gallon plastic container full of water is used to simulate the effect on a person's head of being shot with a cartridge containing 'SG' pellets. It is ripped apart by the impact and its contents explode showering those standing several metres away.

Throughout training the emphasis is upon avoiding direct confrontation unless it is absolutely necessary. Officers are told of the dangers of trying to burst in and catch a wanted person off his guard. For example, the course the author attended was told of how a wanted man, Toni Baldessare, had fortified his flat and had intended to kill as many police officers as possible when they stormed in to arrest him. Fortunately, he was frustrated by the caution shown by the arresting officers who laid siege to his flat for two days before he shot and killed himself.

The dangers of such confrontations extend not only to the police officer, but also to innocent people who may inadvertently become involved. The case of Mrs. Cherry Groce, mistakenly shot during an early morning raid in 1985 by officers searching for her son, was pointed to as tragic evidence of the dangers inherent in this type of operation. This lesson is reinforced by a session on a specially constructed range where photographs are projected onto a screen and the trainee must decide whether to shoot or not. This is a rudimentary piece of equipment, but still allows the lesson to be learned that it is very easy to misinterpret an innocuous action as threatening and to shoot where there was no just cause.

Throughout the course emphasis is repeatedly placed on systematic caution. This is reinforced by a series of practical exercises dealing with various types of armed incident: an armed person in a house, stopping armed persons in a vehicle, and staging an 'ambush' of an armed robber at the scene of the robbery. If officers fail to act in the correct fashion, instructors who act as the suspects in these exercises, deliberately behave in unexpected ways. Many of the exercises are videotaped and later replayed to show the mistakes that trainees actually make in practice. As instructors acknowledge, this does no more than caution trainees against over-hasty action, rather than establish their competence in actually dealing with complex situations.

A good example of the importance of taking a cautious approach is in how officers are taught to take the surrender of an armed person. The great danger in such a situation is that officers will relax, thinking the whole episode is finished and the threat eliminated. Trainees are shown news film showing an actual surrender where the attention of surrounding officers quite clearly diminishes dramatically. It is emphasised that even if it is believed that, say, only one person is involved and he has surrendered, officers can never be sure that premises or vehicles are safe until they have been properly searched and their safety verified. Thus, a surrender is not taken in full view of premises or vehicles that have not been searched. Instead the person is taken to a safe location where he can be searched without being overlooked.

When it comes to searching the person, trainees are again shown the importance of caution and being thorough. If a person is carrying a gun when he emerges, they are shown how he should be directed to hold it so that it cannot quickly be turned on them and fired. The speed with which this can be done is demonstrated and trainees are reminded to remain behind protective cover. Armed persons should not be told to drop their gun, in the manner so often seen on the screen, because this can be sufficient to cause them to discharge and again this is demonstrated. The person is instructed to place the gun carefully on the ground at an appointed place well away from the premises or vehicle from which he has emerged and away from where he will be eventually searched.

If possible the person is made to lie face down with arms and legs spreadeagled and to look in the opposite direction to that from which the searching officer will approach him. Before approaching, the officer will instruct the person to interlace his fingers behind his back and pull his hands as far up his back as possible. The officer then takes hold of the interlaced fingers, preventing the person letting go and slight pressure can cause sufficient pain to inhibit any threatening move. Handcuffs are then applied and the person's entire body thoroughly searched for hidden weapons. During exercises involving the surrender of armed persons, weapons are deliberately hidden in the most unlikely places to test the thoroughness with which trainees search the person. Then the person is assisted to his feet in a particular manner so as to retain control over his movements. In demonstrations instructors show the danger that can arise from sudden and unexpected actions on the part of a person who has apparently surrendered. The emphasis is upon guarding against the unanticipated danger: 'What if ...?'.

This same caution is paramount in dealing with each of the tactical situations with which officers are taught to deal - the barricaded armed criminal in a building, armed persons in vehicles and armed robbers at the scene of a robbery.

a) *Barricaded armed person in a building.*
   The type of armed operation which is most common is that involving people who barricade themselves within a building and have possibly taken a hostage. Typically the person or persons concerned may be criminals who have been disturbed and sought refuge in a building, or a party to a violent 'domestic' quarrel who is holding other members of the family hostage. In any event the task of the police is to contain the building and seek to negotiate the surrender of the person concerned. During training, officers are required to deal with simulated situations of this kind, during which instructors entice them into making premature attempts to rescue hostages or otherwise expose themselves to danger. The lesson is that officers must be patient and not take precipitate action.

Once the person has surrendered and any hostages liberated, the premises must be searched. This is undertaken by a team of officers who methodically and cautiously search each room in turn, maintaining as much silence as possible. Only when each room, including cupboards and lofts or cellars, have been searched and declared safe can others be allowed in, for example, to search for evidence.

b) *Armed Persons in Vehicles*

Another common armed operation is to stop and arrest suspected armed persons in a vehicle. Since the vehicle is likely to be on the public highway, officers are instructed in how to bring it to a halt without exposing members of the public to unnecessary danger. Once halted the occupants of the vehicle must alight in an orderly manner whilst officers maintain as much cover as possible. To this end officers are shown how to position their own vehicle so as to afford maximum protection and how to instruct occupants to behave so as to minimise danger to all concerned. Thus, occupants will be instructed to display both hands and to leave the doors open as each of them alights, at the command of the police, in turn. The last occupant will be instructed to open the boot of the car before joining his colleagues lying face down in the road. Then officers will visually inspect the car from behind cover to ensure that no one remains within it, before the occupants are approached, searched and arrested.

c) *Intercepting Armed Robbers*

Perhaps the most dangerous type of armed operation that an AFO will be called upon to undertake is the interception of armed robbers at the scene of a robbery. Before such an interception (or 'ambush' as it is more colloquially known) can occur, senior officers must assure themselves that it is based on sound intelligence and the Force Firearms Unit must be consulted. Usually, one or more AFOs will accompany members of the Robbery Squad, or other specialist squad, who are responsible for the investigation. At the critical moment when the robbers move in to attack the victim, the police will intercept and capture them. It is the task of the AFO to confront, contain and, if possible, take the surrender of any armed members of the gang. The operation will have been planned in advance, but as officers under training are made aware, operations rarely go entirely according to plan. In the rapidly unfolding circumstances of the operation, in which innocent people are almost inevitably involved, the officer is bound to make split-second decisions, particularly concerning whether to open fire or not.

Basic training has been dealt with at length because this is both the foundation for all further training and also the full extent of initial training received by most AFOs, who comprise the majority of officers authorised to carry firearms.

Reclassification

Four times annually AFOs and all other authorised officers must satisfy the standards of marksmanship required to maintain authorisation. Officers attend at a variety of ranges situated throughout the Metropolitan Police District where they spend some time in practice and the remainder being tested on their marksmanship. Where changes have been introduced, either in procedures or training, these are explained to officers and discussed with them. Thus, following the report of the Home Office Working Party (1986a) changes were introduced regarding the abolition of single-action shooting and weak-hand shooting. These were explained by instructors and discussed with officers reclassifying during the first three months of 1987, when the author was observing reclassification procedures.

Officers also receive additional training to improve techniques in conformity to changing standards. For example, it was decided to require officers to wear a uniform tunic or jacket and draw their weapon from the holster and fire it 'sense of direction' during reclassification. Formerly, officers were trained to aim and fire from the 'drawn weapons position', that is, with the gun drawn from the holster and held ready in front of the body, pointing towards the target. This was on the assumption that officers would normally be prepared for an armed encounter and very rarely be caught off-guard. However, if officers were to be taught to draw from the holster and fire, it was necessary that they should do so wearing the clothing they would wear operationally. Thus, following this policy change, part of the day spent attending for reclassification during the first three months of 1987 involved some retraining in techniques of drawing the gun from the holster beneath a tunic or jacket and firing 'sense of direction'.

Following this period of instruction and training, officers are then tested. The tests do not follow a standard pattern, but are designed to present to officers previously unencountered situations for them to cope with, the aim being to test how well officers adapt. It is impossible, therefore, to describe in detail what occurs at all reclassification tests, so one such test, conducted in March 1987, will be described. It consisted of a total of forty rounds fired in three shoots. The first required officers to be seated and to stand and fire a pair of shots 'sense of direction' at a turning target seven metres distant, exposed for three seconds. The second involved the target at 15 metres being exposed briefly (a 'flash exposure'), whereupon officers were required to draw their gun and shout a warning. When the target reappeared for a total of four seconds they were to fire a pair of aimed shots. Both of these first two shoots were each of ten rounds, thus requiring officers to reload with four rounds having expended the first six. The final test involved firing four rounds standing, four kneeling, four sitting, four kneeling and four standing at a target 25 metres distant in two minutes. Between each set of four shots the expended rounds were to be discarded and the gun topped up with live rounds.

Annual Refresher Training

Each year AFOs must attend a one day refresher training course at the firearms training establishment at Lippitt's Hill. Officers must demonstrate that they are still physically fit by completing a short assault course, then carrying a dummy weighing eleven stones and then holding a gun steady in the aim for one minute. This is a repetition of what is now required for the basic course, but not all AFOs had previously to satisfy this requirement and an annual retest was only introduced at the beginning of 1987.

The remainder of the day is given over to improving skills on the practice range and, more importantly, refreshing and improving tactical knowledge through exercises similar to those completed as part of the basic course.

Training of Officers Using Special Weapons

Before AFOs can be authorised to carry either the Browning 9mm or the Heckler and Koch MP5, they must complete additional training. They also attend reclassification tests once per month and are required to satisfy more demanding examinations of their marksmanship. For example, officers authorised to carry Brownings must engage more than one target, sometimes positioned at different distances, which in aimed shooting requires some refocusing of the eye. Those on the Heckler and Koch MP5 reclassification engage in exercises such as requiring them to walk around as they might in a terminal building and then fire at a target which turns; or to be seated behind a check-in desk and have to shoot one of six targets as nominated by the instructor; or to 'fend off' another person whilst firing single-handed. They must also learn what action to take if their weapon jams, which involves discarding the Heckler and Koch MP5 and drawing and firing their back-up side arm. Since these officers are a small group from within the Heathrow Airport Security Section, this comprises a correspondingly small training commitment.

Training Protection Officers

Officers from the Royalty and Diplomatic Protection Department, responsible for protecting embassies and VIPs, receive an additional three week course designed to teach them the skills and knowledge needed in their role. These include higher standards of marksmanship involving shooting with one hand whilst protecting 'the principal' (the person they are protecting) with the other, or blocking an attack with one arm and firing with the other hand. Some, highly selected, officers also learn how to fire the Heckler and Koch MP5K.

Again, equal attention is paid to tactical considerations. Thus officers are shown how to deploy themselves around a 'principal' and what to do should an attack take place. There are staged exercises in which attempts are made on the life of a 'principal', for example, as the party arrive at a location by car. Officers are taught how to get the 'principal' out of the line of fire and return fire, if necessary. The assessment of situations and liaison with other divisions within the Metropolitan Police or other police forces also commands considerable attention.

'Level II' Training

Competition for recruitment to the 18 'Level II' team positions, newly-established in the Autumn of 1986, was intense, with only 34 of more than 70 applicants being accepted for training. This lasted three weeks and was residential at Lippitt's Hill. Here applicants completed a demanding schedule of classroom tuition and gruelling practical exercises. Of the 34 accepted for training only 21 eventually passed.

In addition to initial training, 'Level II' officers are supposed to train whilst not on operational duties, the aim being to maintain a highly skilled cadre of officers who can relieve AFOs of the more dangerous and difficult tasks such as house searching and taking the surrender of armed persons. They will normally be called in once AFOs have contained an armed person and are often called out to undertake planned arrests of suspected armed offenders, where a slow search of the premises is likely to prove necessary.

'Level I' Training

Not only must 'Level I' officers provide the response to incidents requiring special weapons and tactics, they must also train all other officers in the force authorised to carry any particular weapon. Hence their training requires them to qualify at the highest standard on all the weapons used by police. They must also satisfy demanding standards of physical fitness, including being able to complete an assault course wearing respirators. Finally, they must also show themselves competent in and able to instruct others about the rules and procedures governing police use of firearms.

'Level I' officers follow a six-week cycle: four weeks of instructional duty at either Lippitt's Hill or one of the ranges in and around London is followed by a week's team training and then a week's operational standby. In addition, 'Level I' officers liaise with other police forces and the SAS Special Operations Group, engaging in occasional joint exercises in preparation for an incident such as the Iranian Embassy siege in which both police and SAS were involved.

'Level I' officers are trained to undertake all the operations undertaken by AFOs, but in addition are also trained for the more dangerous task of armed raids on premises. With the growth of organised drug-pushing, there has been a commensurate growth in the frequency with which premises are raided and where the occupants are believed to be armed. Because the purpose of the raid is to secure evidence, and because drugs are easily disposed of, it is essential that officers gain rapid access to the premises. Consequently, officers must burst in and possibly confront suspected armed persons who are intent on delaying them, at least.

In addition to raids of this kind, 'Level I' teams are also trained to undertake hostage rescue. This involves the added danger that the hostage or hostages will be harmed during the assault. Speed is therefore even more essential and familiarity with the use of distraction grenades and CS gas is equally necessary. Given that CS gas may be used in an assault, 'Level I' teams must also be trained to operate whilst wearing respirators. Typically, this kind of operation will not have had the benefit of pre-planning and, therefore, on arrival the team leader will need to formulate a plan of assault should it prove necessary. At the earliest opportunity he will devise an 'immediate action plan' which caters for a sudden deterioration in the situation dictating the need for an assault (such as hostages being killed). Once that is completed, he will turn to a more carefully considered alternative, relying upon better information - the 'deliberate action plan'. Of course, all armed officers must accept that if innocent people are placed in immediate danger they may have to take whatever unplanned action is possible to minimise loss of life or injury.

Conclusions

Training in the use of firearms by the police is now taken more seriously than at any time in the history of the Metropolitan Police. All officers who are authorised to carry firearms are trained in marksmanship skills and tactical awareness. Those who are given more onerous operational responsibilities receive additional training. Whether this is satisfactory enough is just one of the issues that will be discussed in the second part of this report.

Part Two

Issues and Problems

CHAPTER FIVE

THE PEOPLE FOR THE JOB?

Introduction

The practice of carrying firearms is so obviously alien to the British police tradition, that it is not surprising that it has provoked a number of issues. Foremost amongst these are questions regarding the number of officers authorised to carry firearms and their fitness for doing so. These questions have been raised following each of the tragedies concerning the shootings of Stephen Waldorf, John Shorthouse and Cherry Groce. However, wider issues have also been raised about the kind of weapons used, especially the sub-machine guns at Heathrow Airport. Other issues, though no less important, have received less public attention. The following chapters will consider each of these problems.

The Numbers Game

A matter of recurring concern is the actual number of officers who are authorised to carry firearms and the frequency with which those firearms are actually carried (see GLC 1984, Blom-Cooper's evidence to the Home Office Working Party [Home Office 1986a], and Benn and Worpole 1986). Much of this concern seems to have been fuelled by an uncritical acceptance of the figures (reproduced as Figure 1 and Table 1) contained in an M.Sc. dissertation written by a serving police officer (Hoare 1980).

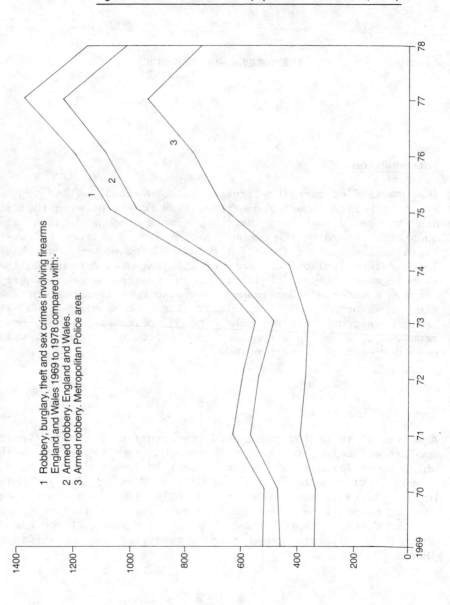

Figure 1: Armed crime 1969-78 (reproduced from Hoare, 1980).

1 Robbery, burglary, theft and sex crimes involving firearms
  England and Wales 1969 to 1978 compared with:-
2 Armed robbery. England and Wales.
3 Armed robbery. Metropolitan Police area.

Table 1   **Police use of firearms compared to armed crime 1970-78.**
Collation of data contained in Hoare (1980)

Year	Issue of guns		Met	Firearms crime		Armed Robbery
	Met	Provinces	as %	Total	Serious	Total*
1970	803	269	75	1,358	524	47,888
1971	1,344	591	69	1,734	633	63,333
1972	1,712	525	77	2,070	599	53,999
1973	-	-	-	2,466	549	48,777
1974	-	-	-	2,828	716	65,000
1975	2,863	1,689	63	3,850	1,069	95,888
1976	4,414	1,953	69	4,632	1,189	107,666
1977	3,933	1,814	68	5,302	1,371	123,444
1978	5,835	1,627	78	5,672	1,138	99,666

*These figures were obtained from *Criminal Statistics England and Wales 1980*, Cmnd. 8376, HMSO, London.

Hoare concludes:

> It is no surprise that the Metropolitan Police averages 76% of the national total of issues, but they are now seen to be breaking steeply away from what appears as an established equilibrium in the rest of the country. This rise does not coincide in any way with known armed crime, but it is likely that a good deal of this upsurge is due to terrorist activity in London.

Others have concluded that these figures simply show a lack of firm control and supervision on the part of the Metropolitan

Police (Benn and Worpole 1986; Blom-Cooper in Home Office 1986a, and Rusbridger 1985).

Hoare performed the very valuable service of exposing deficiencies in the official statistics relating to firearms offences. These, he demonstrated, included both relatively trivial offences of criminal damage and assault caused by youngsters using air weapons and much more serious offences such as armed robbery (Hoare 1980, ch 7). Through a careful re-analysis of the data, Hoare was able to distinguish between the trivial and the serious and we remain indebted to him for this. It is a distinction that the official statistics now also incorporate (Home Office 1986b). Unfortunately, in other respects Hoare gave a misleading interpretation of the data.

Let us begin by considering the claim that the number of firearms issued to Metropolitan Police officers is 'breaking steeply away from what appears as an established equilibrium in the rest of the country'. In addition to Hoare's original data, Figure 0 also provides the number of 'issues' in the Metropolitan Police expressed as a percentage of the national total. This contradicts the suggestion that the Metropolitan Police figures are 'breaking steeply away' from the rest of the country. In fact, throughout the 1970s they formed a U-curve, from roughly three-quarters at the beginning of the decade, dropping to two-thirds during its middle years and rising again to just over three-quarters by the end of the period. The confusion seems to have arisen from the failure to appreciate the difference between the *absolute numbers* of guns issued by the Metropolitan and other police forces and the question of their proportionality. As in any escalating trend, a constant proportional difference produces an increasing absolute difference.

Next, let us consider the view that the increase in firearms issued to police did 'not coincide in any way with known armed crime' (Hoare 1980, p 74). If this was in fact true, there would be no statistical correlation between the number of armed robberies (the single offence accounting for the vast majority of 'serious armed crimes' and for which there are reliable figures) and the number of firearms issued to police. The absence of such a correlation is computed as 0, whereas if

- 50 -

there was a perfect correlation (such that every increase in armed crime was matched by an increase in police firearms issued) the correlation coefficient would have a value of 1.0. In fact, the correlation between the trend in serious armed crime, as defined by Hoare, and the trend in the issue of firearms to Metropolitan Police officers was .85, and that between armed robberies and the issue of police firearms was .79. The comparable figure for the police outside of London was .97 in relation to both serious offences and armed robberies. There was, in short, an extremely close relationship between the occurrence of serious armed crime and the issue of firearms to police.

Again, the reason for this error would seem to be a failure to distinguish between absolute numbers and a *proportional* relationship in an escalating trend. In this case, Hoare compares the *number* of armed offences to the *number* of occasions upon which firearms were issued to individual officers. Both were increasing during the 1970s, but because the number of police firearms issued in the Metropolitan District increased from 803 in 1970 to 5,835 in 1978 and serious firearms offences rose from 524 to 1,138 during the same period, the size of gap obscures the similar trend.

Nevertheless, the question remains: why are there so many firearms issued to police compared to the number of serious armed offences? First, it should be appreciated that this question does not compare like with like: a serious armed offence may involve a number of offenders using firearms, whereas the issue of police firearms refers to a gun being issued to an officer. Thus, even if it was considered unexceptionable that each serious armed offence should provoke the issuing of police firearms, then at least twice as many police weapons would be issued as the number of offences, since the policy is that AFOs should always be deployed in pairs to give each other cover. Second, if police were searching for several armed persons who together had committed one offence, then obviously the number of guns issued to individual officers may increase accordingly. Third, if an armed operation persisted over a number of days, then the number of guns issued would also increase accordingly. For example, the recent incident at the Sir John Soane's Museum, when an armed robber was shot and killed, had involved four armed officers waiting for three days to intercept these armed men (*Police Review* 12 February 1987). Under the procedures appertaining during the 1970s, this would have amounted to twelve 'issues'. Thus, it is virtually inevitable that firearms issued to police will outnumber armed robberies to a considerable degree. It was to prevent erroneous conclusions, such as these, being drawn from the published figures, that the basis for calculating the use of police firearms was changed in 1983 from the number of guns issued to individual officers to the number of 'armed operations'. Under this system the 'stakeout' at the Sir John Soane's Museum would have constituted a single 'operation'. However, it is unfortunate that official figures on the total number of guns issued are not longer available, since this would give the most complete picture.

Even had Hoare's interpretation of the data been correct, it is far from clear whether it would indicate anything like the 'Starsky and Hutch syndrome' of which the police have been accused (Rusbridger 1985). As Hoare's figures on serious armed crime show (Hoare 1980, pp 46-54), there was a qualitative change in the mid-1970s towards a greatly increased use of firearms, especially shotguns (p 52). A shotgun loaded with 'SG' - that is nine .30" pellets - is a particularly lethal weapon, as police firearms training is at pains to point out (see above p 34). As the use of such weapons became much more prevalent during the 1970s (see Hoare 1980), so officers would quite reasonably take the obvious precaution of carrying weapons with which to defend themselves and others whenever there was reason to believe that they might encounter armed criminals. To use an analogy, it is not surprising that the blood transfusion service responded to the AIDS epidemic by screening *all* blood products, despite the small number of people who have been found to be carrying the HIV virus. Nor is it surprising that one bomb, killing five people at the Conservative Party Conference, prompted a huge security operation for all subsequent party conferences. Whilst either of these responses could be portrayed as statistically disproportionate to the scale of the risk, neither of them in fact are, because in both cases the risk has increased *qualitatively*. The growth in armed crime during the 1970s shows a similar qualitative change. What is surprising is not that the police now issue firearms much more frequently than they did in the past, but that their use of firearms has remained so closely related to the incidence of serious armed crime.

Whether justified or not, the police have responded to public concern about the number of AFOs and the procedures for issuing firearms by gradually reducing the former and strengthening the latter. In 1983, following the 'Dear Report' into the mistaken shooting of Stephen Waldorf, the level at which authorisation could be granted was raised to that of Commander rank, thus making it more difficult to issue firearms, even at the risk of possible delay. The Home Office Working Party (1986a) took some comfort from the gradual reduction in the number of AFOs and armed operations in recent years. The Commissioner of the Metropolitan Police announced that the number of AFOs in his force was being reduced and that no longer would divisional CID be authorised to carry firearms. On the other hand, in the wake of the Hungerford massacre there has been criticism of the reduction in the numbers of armed police on the grounds that they are insufficient to provide a swift response to such an incident (Edwards 1988). Perhaps the lesson to be drawn from this controversy is that in this regard the police simply cannot 'win' (Waddington 1988).

Selection and Training

Another issue that has frequently been raised in connection with the police use of firearms, is the adequacy of selection and the quality of training. Concern has been expressed about the ability of armed officers to perform satisfactorily under the acute stress that is bound to accompany an armed operation. There seems to be a fear that volunteers for the position of AFO will be people unhealthily attracted to guns. Some faith seems to have been placed in the use of psychometric tests to discover which officers have a healthy attitude towards firearms and to predict how they will respond to stress. Unfortunately, after experimenting with several possible psychometric tests, the Home Office Working Party concluded (Home Office 1986a) that none had proven satisfactory. The reason is undoubtedly that it is the situation rather than the character or temperament of an individual officer that is the principal determinant of behaviour in armed operations, as in so many areas of human activity.

Currently, selection occurs at two levels: the commander of the division or squad must first satisfy himself that officers sent for training have proven themselves suitable, and instructors must also be satisfied as to the suitability of the trainee. If at any time an officer's suitability comes into question his authorisation is withdrawn. Despite the fact that these are subjective judgements, they seem more likely to be reliable than psychometric tests which, at best, can only consider a few variables.

From the opposite point of view, it has been suggested that the concern to avoid selecting people with an 'unhealthy' interest in firearms actually militates against the selection of suitable individuals. Yardley and Eliot (1986b) claim that officers 'will be actively discouraged from private firearms ownership' with the result that they will only gain familiarity in handling weapons during their periodic refresher training (see also Yardley and Eliot 1986c). Whether or not forces outside the Metropolitan Police adopt such a policy cannot be affirmed or denied here, but certainly it is the case that many instructors and AFOs in the Metropolitan Police belong to gun clubs and there is a long tradition of recreational shooting organised by the Metropolitan Police Sports and Social Clubs (Gould and Waldren 1986).

The unsupported allegation that the police avoid selecting officers with a sporting interest in firearms, detracts from the more serious point made by Yardley and Eliot (1986a), namely that compared to the training given to drivers of police vehicles the length of time devoted to training AFOs is grossly inadequate. A basic driving course lasts four weeks and most drivers will have the opportunity to practise some of their driving skills, at least, on a daily basis. AFOs, on the other hand, receive a basic course of ten days (and prior to

1983 it lasted only five days) and have the opportunity to
practise officially four days per year. Indeed, it seems that
only successive tragedies have wrenched the necessary
resources from the authorities to extend training even to this
meagre ration. It took the murder of three unarmed detectives
in 1966 for the police to abandon 'amateurism' and begin
systematic training at all. It was the Waldorf shooting which
prompted a major internal inquiry - the 'Dear Report' -
resulting in extended training being given to officers. The
shootings of John Shorthouse and Mrs. Groce likewise provoked
a major review and innovations such as 'Level II' teams.

The use of firearms is not established as part of the police
function in the way that driving emergency vehicles has
become, nor have problems arisen with sufficient frequency to
demonstrate that this is a task which demands lengthy
training. Thus, in the competition for resources, immediately
pressing demands such as for improved riot training, seem to
predominate. Firearms training only becomes a pressing issue
in the wake of some incident which throws its adequacy into
question.

Certainly the resource implications of firearms training are
considerable. There is a total of 56 officers engaged full-
time in firearms training in the Metropolitan Police. In 1986
the training commitment amounted to 19,630 man-days for
officers who would otherwise be available for other duties. In
line with the 'Dear Report', the force intends to double the
amount of refresher training from four to eight days annually
and this will add a further 7,500 man-days to that total.
Added to this is the cost of practice ammunition, targets,
building and maintaining ranges, testing instructors for the
level of lead in their blood and much more besides. The annual
budget for firearms training during the year 1985-86 amounted
to approximately £2 million. Thus, it is not difficult to
appreciate the resistance to committing further resources in
view of the government's financial management initiative which
insists upon showing tangible benefits resulting from
expenditure. Furthermore, there is the laudable desire not to
take officers away from street duties unnecessarily. Thus, the
proposal contained in the Dear Report to extend refresher
training to eight days per annum has only begun to be

introduced and will be gradually phased in, because of its financial implications. It is partly in order to maintain control over the size of the training commitment that the number of authorised officers has been reduced, so that henceforth they will be fewer but better trained.

There is no doubt that training has improved substantially since 1966 nor is there much doubt that training in the Metropolitan Police compares favourably with that provided by other forces in Britain or overseas. However, there is equally no doubt that much room exists for improvement, particularly in standards of marksmanship and tactics, at both initial and refresher training levels. During initial training officers are taught to fire their weapon at a static paper target on a practice range in good light. They repeat the same 'shoot' usually ten times and will know for how long the target will be exposed. For only one brief session they are presented with still photographs portraying a variety of actual scenes which require them to consider whether or not to shoot. There is no opportunity for officers to be presented with simulated incidents in which moving targets have to be distinguished from innocent bystanders under varying conditions of light and heat. Plans are in hand to install a sophisticated simulator which will present complex scenarios in which officers will need to decide whether or not to shoot. If this simulator was installed in a suitable vehicle it could be taken to the stations from which AFOs worked and allow them to gain regular practice more cheaply than sending them to some fixed location. However, even this technology is limited, for whilst the scenarios can be changed so as to avoid familiarity, they are played out no matter what action the officer takes short of opening fire. He is a passive observer of circumstances until he decides to shoot.

Attempts are made by instructors within their limited resources to improve marksmanship skills during refresher training. Officers are increasingly exposed to tests which require them to be seated, or to walk around, or fend off an imaginary bystander, or to shout a warning. The ingenuity shown by instructors in devising these tests within the constraints they face is laudable. However, for a Heckler and Koch MP5 trained officer to be faced with six targets, one of which is nominated by the instructor for him to engage, is a far cry from confronting one or more terrorists in a crowded terminal building.

Yardley and Eliot (1986b) have argued for more realistic training involving officers engaging other people with wax bullets which inflict minor injuries but are not lethal. They have gone further and suggested that some training exercises should involve the use of live rounds to simulate the experience of genuine combat. These suggestions were rejected by the Home Office Working Party on the grounds that they laid too much emphasis on 'engagement' rather than 'containment' (Home Office 1986a). This is a reasonable argument, for police officers are not soldiers and a successful strategy is designed to ensure that there is a peaceful conclusion to the incident not a shoot-out. However, whilst this is generally true there are some officers who might need to engage armed persons. These include officers at Heathrow Airport who might find themselves in an exchange of fire with terrorists. Indeed, equipping them with the Heckler and Koch MP5 carbine is justified precisely on the grounds of their possibly needing to engage terrorists. Much the same seems to apply to officers in the Royalty and Diplomatic Protection Department. For these officers, at least, there might be some merit in training along the lines suggested by Yardley and Eliot (1986b).

On the other hand, the Working Group was surely correct in insisting that for the vast majority of officers the emphasis should be upon 'containment' rather than 'engagement'. If officers avoid confrontations, so that they do not need to distinguish between when and when not to shoot under conditions of extreme stress, then this is much more likely to ensure that innocent people are not mistakenly shot. However well-trained and mentally stable a person might be, there is always the possibility that in making a split-second decision they will do so in error. Adequate tactical training avoids the futile quest for a cadre of superhuman individuals to whom firearms can be entrusted.

However, given the emphasis upon 'containment' rather than 'engagement', the amount of time devoted to tactical training seems inadequate. The basic course includes a number of tactical exercises in containment, the interception of vehicles and 'ambushing' armed robbers. These are of immense value, especially when video taped for later replay to the officers concerned to whom mistakes can be pointed out. However, the opportunities for such tactical exercises, even during a two-week course are limited. Trainees are not brought up to a standard of proficiency, they are simply shown how *deficient* they are in the hope that given this knowledge they will exhibit caution in actual operations. This would be less regrettable if subsequent refresher training included tactical exercises designed to build upon the basic training. Unfortunately, this only occurs during the *annual* refresher course, because there is neither time nor facilities for doing this on a tri-monthly basis.

Effective tactics are no less difficult to teach than is marksmanship, because tactical training must overcome the strong imperative felt by officers to intervene - to 'do something' to resolve the situation immediately. It is this imperative which leads to many mistakes in training and potentially in practice. Officers are disinclined to surround premises and wait as a gunman utters threats against unseen hostages. The imperative is to form a 'raid group' and enter the premises even at substantial risk to themselves and possibly to innocent people. Only frequent training exercises in which the techniques of containment are rehearsed can be expected to counteract this tendency, but at present this is not available.

Not only is refresher training insufficient to provide adequate rehearsal of tactics, it is also insufficient for the maintenance of simple marksmanship skills. A three month lapse during which an officer might not even have handled a gun is a lengthy period. The sheer familiarity with the weapon shows a noticeable deterioration during this time. For example, when reloading with a 'part load' (that is, less than six rounds in the cylinder) it is necessary to position the chambers so that when the trigger is pulled and the cylinder rotates the first loaded chamber moves into line with the barrel. Thus, the cylinder must be closed with the last empty chamber aligned with the barrel and not with a loaded chamber in this position because it will rotate when the trigger is squeezed. This is a rudimentary handling skill, but one which can be forgotten in the period between refresher courses. It is of no great significance on a practice range where instructors can remind the officer of this point, but if an officer was called out on an armed operation shortly before his refresher training was due, this kind of handling problem could have serious consequences.

Thus, although training has improved considerably in recent years there seems to be much more that can be done. Senior officers concerned with firearms training are acutely aware that this is so, but are constrained by budgetary restrictions. Certainly, the cost implications of substantial improvements in training will be considerable. Capital expenditure would be necessary for the construction of a central London training complex in which tactical exercises could be mounted. The drain on manpower due to the commitments for regular refresher training would also be enormous. What the Metropolitan Police and the Home Office must balance is the cost of less than complete competence against the likely gain from greatly improved training, especially tactical training. Given that one bungled operation can spark a riot and do immeasurable harm to the reputation of the police, apart from causing death or injury to innocent persons, it would seem that a substantial improvement in training is needed to restore that balance.

Generalists or Specialists?

One way of trying to achieve some balance between costs and rewards is to concentrate resources upon a relatively small group of people who can be highly trained. This seems to be the direction in which policy on firearms has been moving during recent years. The Home Office Working Party report of 1986 certainly endorsed such a move and in the Metropolitan Police this took the form of establishing the 'Level II' teams.

The advantages of specialisation are clear enough: a small

group of officers can be removed from general policing commitments and dedicated to firearms training and operations, ensuring the highest standards of competence. Also the same officers work together as a team thereby coming to know each other's capabilities and acquiring trust in one another, so that they can act as a cohesive unit rather than a collection of individuals. Their frequent exposure to operational conditions familiarises them with the vagaries of actual operations so that they are less likely to be caught off-guard. Elite status raises morale and can become an incentive for maintaining strict discipline. All of these advantages have been demonstrated by the Force Firearms Unit itself over the years.

Equally, there are evident disadvantages in specialisation: an inevitable corollary is that a limited number of officers will be placed repeatedly in the position of having to confront armed criminals and terrorists. Apart from the risk to which this exposes such officers, it also means that these few officers will be repeatedly called upon to decide whether to open fire or not. Whilst such highly trained men may be best able to make this decision, it does place an enormous burden upon few shoulders and exposes them also to accusations that they are 'gun happy' if, and when, they decide to open fire, particularly if they do so on more than one occasion.

Greenwood (1986) has complained that it marginalises firearms within the police context, encouraging a lack of familiarity with weapons and exposing police and civilians alike to incompetent use of firearms by non-specialist police officers. It is also an expensive use of scarce resources of manpower, for despite the increased frequency of armed operations in London during the recent past, they are not so frequent as to employ a team of officers full-time. Non-operational time can be profitably used for team training, but even this may not occupy them adequately. Thus, when establishing 'Level II' teams it was decided to abandon the initial proposal to have one such team in each of the force's eight territorial Areas. Also since many operations require trained and disciplined officers to work as a team, but do not need the very highest levels of expertise, 'Level II' officers are trained only to use the standard model 10 revolver. The use of special weapons and more advanced tactics remains the province of the 'Level I' officers.

However, there are limitations upon how much specialisation there can be. If all armed operations were to be undertaken by 'Level II' teams they would need to be vastly expanded, because although armed operations are few in number, they often occur concurrently. For example, it is usually safest and most convenient to arrest wanted people early in the morning when few innocent bystanders are about and the person is located in identified premises. A number of such 'early morning calls' may occur at or around the same time, requiring several teams of armed officers. In addition, other teams would need to remain on standby in case any other armed incident was to occur. Moreover, to be readily available to respond to armed incidents, especially those occurring spontaneously, teams would need to be distributed throughout London.

For these reasons it is unlikely that the Metropolitan Police (still less any other British police force) will adopt the full-time dedicated firearms teams, similar to the Special Weapons and Tactics Teams (SWATs), common in American cities, advocated by Yardley and Eliot (1986c). It seems probable that the most highly skilled officers will continue to act also as instructors to the rest of the force. Moreover, there are advantages to be gained from this dual role. Whilst their dual role may be described as 'over-burdening' the Force Firearms Unit 'with other duties, such as teaching other officers basic firearms skills' (Yardley and Eliot 1986c), this combination of an instructional and elite operational role enhances the status of training. When a member of an elite operational squad instructs trainees to give priority to caution and safety, this cannot be dismissed as theoretical advice divorced from operational reality which can be safely disregarded.

It seems inevitable that since the Force Firearms Unit will remain small and not readily available to respond to all armed incidents, at least *some* ordinary police officers will be required to maintain a proficiency in the use of firearms whilst continuing their other duties. If so, these 'Level III' officers should receive more frequent training both on the practice range and in tactics. It is at this level that there continues to be a failure fully to embrace the 'professional' approach and rely upon a measure of 'amateurism'.

Command

Another respect in which amateurism has still to be eradicated, is the command of armed operations. Officers to whom guns are issued will rarely be above the rank of sergeant and will, therefore, be subordinated to the decisions of unarmed senior officers who plan the operation or assume command once it has begun. Whereas the AFO at the scene will have received possibly two weeks' initial training and regular refresher training, the senior officer who commands him may be, and in the past frequently has been, wholly untrained.

Amongst AFOs there circulates a host of horror stories concerning what senior officers have commanded armed officers to do. For example, it is alleged that in one incident an armed intruder was thought to be in a house and so two AFOs attended, along with two dog-handlers. After a brief wait during which no activity could be seen within the house, the senior officer formed two pairs comprising an AFO and dog-handler in each. He then instructed one pair to enter through the front door and the other through the rear to search the premises. Thereby, he violated firearms policy on several counts: he needlessly placed officers in a situation which might have resulted in a confrontation with an armed criminal in which they or he or some innocent person might have been shot; he sent a search group in without either a support group or cover group; he instructed them to enter through separate entrances, instead of the same entrance, with the result that they might have suddenly encountered each other in circumstances which could have precipitated an exchange of fire; had the gunman been encountered, say, in the ground floor hallway, and had there been an exchange of fire with him, officers entering from the front might have been firing towards officers entering from the rear and vice versa; and the dogs and their handlers were untrained in working with firearms. Fortunately, the gunman had escaped and nothing untoward occurred. (For another example see Yardley and Eliot 1986c.)

This and other similar stories may, of course, be apocryphal, but gain credibility from what has been publicly revealed about the management of armed operations in cases that have resulted in court action. For example, Steven Waldorf was shot by an officer, DC Finch, who had previously been involved in a life and death struggle with David Martin (the man for whom Waldorf was mistaken) and had been sent alone and without protective cover to look into the yellow mini car being followed by police and confirm whether it was Martin in the passenger seat as suspected. It is hardly any wonder that when he saw a person whom he believed to be Martin make a sudden movement, he panicked and opened fire. In fact, Finch should never have been placed in that situation and certainly he should not have been allowed to go unsupported and without cover possibly to confront a person known to be armed and highly dangerous. Other incidents too have raised equally serious issues about the management of armed operations. The Chief Firearms Instructor said in evidence during the trial of Inspector Lovelock that the operation violated the 'golden rule' of avoiding confrontation (*The Times* 13 January 1987).

Mistakes of this kind occur for several reasons, not least of which is ignorance. Untrained tactical commanders may simply be unaware of the lethality of shotguns - difficult though this might be to comprehend - or the need for armed officers to operate in pairs. Thus, armed operations are conceived and implemented like their unarmed equivalents. The time-hallowed means of arresting wanted persons is to surprise them early in the morning, with a sudden and overwhelming force. To this standard procedure may be added AFOs, to deal with a person who is possibly armed. Thus, the door is opened with a sledgehammer and officers rush in, often with little notion of who, apart from the wanted person, is in the premises and where they are located. What is surprising is not that very occasionally a startled officer fires a shot which kills or injures an innocent person, as happened in the cases of John Shorthouse and Mrs Cherry Groce, but that this happens so rarely.

The Metropolitan Police are aware of this problem and have instituted an urgent programme of senior officer training, designed to inform those who command such operations of the proper tactics to adopt. During the two-day course they are informed of the need to contain a situation and ensure that officers are protected behind suitable cover at an appropriate distance from the threat. The destructive power of the shotgun is demonstrated, so that they do not minimise the risks of such weapons. Trained senior officers, it is hoped, will resist the temptation to opt for an 'early morning turnover' when they suspect the wanted person is armed. Instead, they are advised to contain the premises with a cover group and keep innocent bystanders away with a perimeter group. Only when the situation is secured should they telephone or communicate in some other way with those inside the premises and invite them to surrender. By pursuing the strategy of defensive caution that their AFOs are taught, it is hoped that mistakes can be avoided.

However, it is difficult to disagree with the conclusion of Yardley and Eliot (1986c):

> ... any senior officer who is to command marksmen cannot do that job effectively unless he has some degree of proficiency in, and understanding of, the tactical use of firearms himself. This cannot be accomplished in a course lasting a couple of days. (p 26)

More importantly, perhaps, too much emphasis is being placed upon training and too little attention paid to the way in which the circumstances can often militate against effective command. This can occur in several ways: first, senior commanders need to attend to a wide variety of matters, even in the context of an armed operation, only one of which is the tactical option. The manpower implications of establishing a cover and perimeter group are quite considerable and may have a dramatic impact on the overtime budget for which the senior officer is also responsible. Adopting the correct tactics for an armed operation may severely impede the ability of the local police to discharge other functions, either at the time or later.

Second, although the allocation of resources necessary to ensure safety may be deemed worthwhile if it is *certain* that a suspect is armed, it is frequently the case that whilst there may be a reasonable suspicion that the person is armed, this is not felt at the time to be a sufficiently firm basis upon which to commit the resources necessary for a complete containment. An example of the uncertainty that sometimes faces senior officers who must decide how to deploy their resources occurred during the Christmas holiday of 1986 when a man entered the house of his former cohabitee and fired a shotgun, apparently at her as she escaped and at the two police officers called to the scene. Since the circumstances appeared quite certainly to warrant it, a containment was established using local AFOs, dog handlers and unarmed officers. Moreover, since it also seemed certain that a second man and the woman's two children were being held hostage 'Level I' officers were asked to attend. However, certainty became clouded by growing doubt when, after several hours, it became increasingly apparent that the second man and the children were *not*, in fact, being held hostage. Eventually, the 'Level I' team entered the house, with the assistance of a police dog, to search it. They found a shotgun lying beside the body of a man with shotgun wounds on the ground floor and it was evident that he had been dead for some time. Thus, whilst the senior officer in command of this incident faced what appeared to be a clear hostage-taking incident and responded exactly as he is advised by force policy and training to do, the situation was other than it seemed and the expenditure of resources on the containment proved, with hindsight, to have been unnecessary. Senior officers facing what appear to be much less certain circumstances may well feel that they cannot afford to expend scarce resources to deal with what seems to be only the remote possibility that the situation is more serious than it seems.

Third, in deciding how to deal with an uncertain situation a senior officer may opt for an approach with which he is familiar and has served him well in the past, rather than one that is unfamiliar to him. Although armed operations are becoming increasingly common in the Metropolitan Police

District, compared to the totality of police work they remain the exception. In the experience of a senior officer who, in all probability began his career 20 or more years previously, when armed operations were even more exceptional, such an incident is likely to be an extremely rare occurrence. Perhaps it is only to be anticipated that in such a situation, the familiar approach is preferred to its unfamiliar alternative.

The task of countering all these influences and persuading a senior officer to deal with an armed operation appropriately will, at best, be the responsibility of an AFO acting as a 'tactical adviser', who is almost certainly going to be an officer junior both in rank and experience to the man he is 'advising'. Whilst one must concur with the view that 'a good commander should never be unwilling to ask subordinates for their opinions' (Yardley and Eliot 1986c), this remains a classic example of a contradiction between rank and expertise in an hierarchical organisation. The 'incident commander' is expected to do what his title implies - 'command' - and this may seem inconsistent with accepting the advice and guidance of subordinates.

Moreover, in attempting to persuade a senior officer to adopt the appropriate approach, the AFO (or even a sergeant in charge of a 'Level I' or 'Level II' team) is only one influence amongst many. In a major incident the 'incident commander' may be joined by other senior ranking officers acting as negotiators. They will be able to discuss the situation much more easily as equals, than can a senior officer and his AFO subordinate. Apart from these internal police influences, a senior officer may be influenced by the quite proper desire not to jeopardise relationships that have been forged with the local community by mounting a highly public containment. Amidst all these competing influences a relatively junior officer may find it very difficult to ensure that all the relevant tactical considerations are given due weight by his superiors.

The problems of tactical firearms advice having sufficient influence are just as severe when AFOs join unarmed specialist squads for particular operations, such as an 'ambush' of suspected armed robbers. Here the danger is that the AFO is not a member of the squad and that the armed dimension to the operation is, by virtue of its exceptional quality, treated as peripheral. Tactical advice can be regarded as secondary to the main purpose of the operation, for example, securing the arrest of wanted men. This is particularly evident when AFOs join specialist squads, for example, to intercept armed robbers during a robbery. It seems that the method commonly used by such squads for 'ambushing' robbers not armed with guns, is to 'rush them' with overwhelming force of numbers. Thus, when the command is given, men rush from all directions surprising and over-powering the robbers by superior numbers in what reputedly often degenerates into a melee. However, when the robbers are armed, this approach is highly dangerous. Yet, it is alleged by instructors, and confirmed by film taken covertly by police during actual arrests, and which is used in the training of 'Level II' teams, that frequently, despite planning to the contrary, members of squads continue to 'rush' armed men whilst their AFO colleagues are left somewhat impotent as unarmed officers obscure their line of fire. Such a practice may be given unwitting official approval when unarmed officers acting with foolhardy courage in such circumstances receive awards for bravery.

In the light of all this the complacency of the Home Office Working Party's endorsement of the Manual of Guidance advice is striking. This reads:

> ... a tactical adviser should always be consulted. He should be, or should have been, an authorised firearms officer himself and should have extensive background knowledge of tactical solutions, deployment, communications, and option and contingency planning. The tactical adviser should not himself be part of the operation and may be of *any rank*. (Home Office 1986a, p 12, emphasis added)

The Working Party's recommendation 'that chief officers be reminded of the importance of ensuring that the commanders of armed operations always consult a tactical adviser' also appears insufficiently forceful.

On the other hand, incident commanders may have equal

difficulty in *commanding* those who are expert in such a specialised area as armed operations. This recently came to light during an exercise simulating an armed hostage-taking. A senior officer acting as incident commander found himself suddenly surrounded by a variety of experts, each of whom proceeded with their predetermined task with little reference to him. He felt himself not to be 'in control' of the situation, despite being formally responsible for the actions being taken. In so far as he was asked to make decisions, he lacked the knowledge with which to question them or consider alternatives. The situation itself developed without the incident commander being kept continuously informed.

It would seem that current arrangements are unsatisfactory for all concerned. It is necessary for the safety of members of the public, officers and suspects that the correct command decisions are made at the most appropriate times. It is equally necessary that incident commanders should be able effectively to command an operation for which they are responsible. For these reasons, perhaps armed operations could be commanded along the lines of incidents of major public disorder. In particular, on each of the force's eight Areas a cadre of officers, trained in commanding armed operations, could provide a pool of officers capable of taking command of a major incident in the same way that there are cadres of public order trained senior officers capable of commanding incidents of major disorder. Certainly, the need for competent and effective command is no less important in armed operations than in incidents of serious public disorder.

Legal Liability

The suggestion that at least some senior officers are less than wholly competent in managing armed operations raises the thorny issue of who should be held liable in law when operations go wrong (see Greenwood [1979] ch 2, for a general discussion of the legal position of police using deadly force). At present, as officers are continually reminded during their initial and refresher training, the individual officer is deemed to be responsible for his actions. Thus, it was DCs Finch and Jardine who were tried for the attempted murder of Stephen Waldorf, PC Chester who was tried for the manslaughter of John Shorthouse, and Inspector Lovelock who stood trial for the malicious wounding of Mrs. Groce. In each of these cases it was the officer holding the gun who was held accountable. Yet in each of these cases, serious questions were raised about the management of the operation for which the officer in the dock was not, and should not have been, held responsible.

Of course, officers who use their weapon recklessly must be held responsible for their actions. However, when a senior officer orders a subordinate to enter a situation where he might confront an armed suspect and be required to make a split-second decision whether to shoot or not, it seems unjust for the officer to be required to shoulder the responsibility alone if an innocent person is injured or killed in these circumstances. Unfortunately the response of the authorities to the various incidents which have given rise to public concern has not been to deal effectively with the problem. After the Waldorf shooting, the Home Office issued new guidelines which the Police Federation magazine, *Police* (1983), rightly paraphrased as 'Whitelaw tells police: "You're on your own"'. One does not need to endorse the view of the Police Federation that 'armed officers should have some form of legal protection indemnity from prosecution' (*Police Review* 23 October 1983) to recognise the injustice of heaping such responsibility exclusively upon the shoulders of officers who are unlikely to hold a rank above that of sergeant.

Additional problems regarding the legal liability of armed officers arise from the conservative policy adopted towards armed operations described above. It will be recalled that an officer is instructed to use a firearm only as a last resort in conditions where killing a person could be justified as 'reasonable force' under the Criminal Law Act 1967. Whilst every use of force must be justified as 'reasonable *in the circumstances*' and these circumstances cannot be precisely stipulated in advance, certain problems do recur with sufficient frequency as to demand greater attention. In particular, it sometimes happens that an armed person will refuse to comply with instructions from surrounding officers, perhaps threatening to breach the containment, but not act in such a way as to immediately threaten life.

The difficulties that arise were dramatically illustrated by an incident which occurred in 1979 in Essex. A young man, Paul Howe, with a history of mental disorder took a hostage in an attempt to escape arrest. He and his hostage drove from Chelmsford to Harwich where he boarded and attempted to hijack a cargo ship. Having failed in this attempt, he drove with his hostage to the village of Ramsey where he seized the 'Castle' public house. During this extended chase Howe had several times discharged his shotgun at police and some other hapless road-users, fortunately without causing injury. The police had also had many opportunities of shooting Howe, but had refrained from doing so in the hope of peacefully resolving the situation. Throughout the protracted siege of the public house Howe again fired a number of shots at police, eventually wounding one officer and pinning others in the forward control point to the floor with a fusillade of shots. It was shortly after this, some twelve hours after the incident had begun the previous afternoon, that Howe emerged from the public house carrying a pump-action shotgun. He was challenged to surrender but refused to comply with police instructions. Instead he walked with the gun held across chest towards the surrounding officers, but not, *at that moment*, aiming the gun at any of them. Eventually, a sergeant found himself without cover as Howe walked around the car behind which the officer was sheltering. Faced by a man who had proven himself dangerous and unpredictable and without protection the sergeant opened fire killing Howe.

More recently, in November 1987, Avon and Somerset trapped Glyn Davis in a country lane following a lengthy chase. According to press reports (*Police Review* 27 November 1987), Davis had earlier threatened bailiffs attempting to serve a court order concerning the custody of Davis's three year old daughter and the police who were accompanying them. Davis made off with his daughter and during the ensuing chase threatened pursuing police officers and other members of the public. When cornered, Davis reportedly walked towards armed police, aiming the shotgun and appearing to 'pump' the loading mechanism of his shotgun. Approximately ten yards from the policemen he was shot and killed.

The dilemma in both these instances was essentially the same: should police prevent an armed and dangerous person from breaching the containment, if necessary by shooting him, or should they pull the containment back or allow the gunman through? In each of the incidents described above, the immediate threat posed by the gunman to the officers themselves would probably be regarded as sufficient to warrant use of the 'last resort' of shooting him. However, the Essex and Avon and Somerset police are not alone in facing this kind of dilemma. Incidents have occurred in the Metropolitan Police District in which armed persons have similarly refused to comply and threatened to breach the containment, but fortunately they have eventually been arrested without either shots being fired or the containment breached. There have even been occasions in which unarmed persons, mistakenly believed to be armed, have similarly refused to comply with instructions from surrounding armed officers. It may seem difficult to understand why anyone would put themselves in a position of such obvious jeopardy, but it has become so common in the United States that it is now colloquially referred to as 'suicide by cop'.

If the police responded to these kinds of situations by allowing the gunman or suspected gunman to escape, they may then be held responsible for any death or injury he subsequently inflicted. This was the possibility raised by Mr Justice Mars-Jones during the trial of Hussein Said for the attempted assassination of the Israeli Ambassador, Sholom Argov. The would-be assassin had fired only one shot from his automatic weapon, hitting the Ambassador in the head, when his weapon jammed and he ran off. He was pursued by the Ambassador's protection officer who, having shouted a warning, fired one shot at the escaping gunman, wounding him. During the trial the defence submitted that unnecessary force was used to make the arrest. However, summing up the judge commented that not only did the officer act lawfully and properly in shooting to prevent an armed and dangerous man from escaping, *he would have been neglecting his duty had he not done so* (Gould and Waldren, 1986). Whilst unexceptionable in the circumstances of this case, if this is the law then it places the armed officer in an unenviable position if faced with an armed person who refuses to comply with instructions to lay down his arms and submit to arrest. If he opens fire he may be guilty of using unreasonable force and if he does not he may be guilty of neglecting his duty. Ideally, the situation would not arise because a police dog would assist in making the arrest, but the circumstances may be such that no police dog is available. At the very least, it seems unreasonable to expect officers to shoulder the responsibility that inevitably accompanies the use of firearms in conditions of such apparent legal ambiguity.

Post-Shooting Trauma

A related problem arises when dealing with the aftermath of a shooting, for on the one hand it may be appropriate to suspend the officer concerned from duty, but on the other it may be necessary to avoid any suggestion that he behaved improperly. The need to suspend may be twofold: first, officers involved in shootings frequently suffer what has come to be called in the United States 'post-shooting trauma'. Therefore, such an officer may need a period of intensive counselling to assist him in overcoming this traumatic event. Second, if the shooting is in any way controversial (and rarely are shootings wholly uncontroversial), it may be diplomatic to remove the officer from duty whilst an investigation into the incident is conducted. On the other hand, to *suspend* an officer from duty normally carries overtones of impropriety and may convey the wrong impression to the public and the rest of the police service.

The Metropolitan Police have been actively seeking a solution to this problem, which will routinely involve the suspension of any officer involved in a shooting incident, but avoid any imputation of impropriety on his part. At present an interim solution seems to be to place automatically such an officer on sick leave necessitated by the stress occasioned by the incident. This may turn out to be the most satisfactory solution, since it is virtually inevitable that anyone involved in a shooting incident will be suffering stress and should certainly receive counselling (Manolias and Hyatt-

Williams 1988).

Should Police Be Armed At All?

This chapter has concerned itself so far with problems concerning the numbers of armed police, the training they receive, the frequency with which arms are carried, the adequacy of command and the legal liability of the armed officer. All of this is predicated on the assumption that it is right for at least *some* officers to be armed some of the time. However, this assumption has been radically challenged by Jacobs and Sanders (1986) who conclude that police should not be armed at all. They argue first, that arming the police for their own self-defence transfers the risk of injury, however remote, from the police to innocent third parties. Since there is nothing to choose between an injury to a police officer and injuries to other innocent people, there is no reason to advantage police to the disadvantage of the public. Secondly, they point out that the risk to police officers from armed criminals may be no greater, and possibly less, than the danger to other groups, such as postmasters and security guards. If police have a claim to be armed for their self defence so too do these other groups and this would transform Britain into an armed society like the United States with all the negative consequences that entails. Thirdly, in reply to the argument that the state owes a duty to those upon whom it imposes hazardous responsibilities, they claim that the state owes an equal duty to many other groups of citizens which it discharges with less care than it does its duty to the police. For example, the state does not properly safeguard threatened minorities, whereas it lavishes resources upon law and order. They conclude that:

> ... access to guns is a privilege. A just and democratic society cannot give privileges to one group and withhold them from another unless the first group has a greater right to, or need for, that privilege. At present the police have no greater right to, or need for, firearm protection than countless other groups of people. (Jacobs and Sanders 1986, p 13)

Although this argument will appear to many to be ridiculous (see Waddington 1986), it serves the useful purpose of challenging us to justify why police, and police alone, should be allowed to carry firearms. Such a justification actually obliges us to recognise the reality that police are not merely 'citizens in uniform', but are 'monopolists of force in civil society' with duties that the rest of us do not share. In fact, Jacobs and Sanders acknowledge this when they note:

> Police officers are unusual in that the state places them in jeopardy and does not allow them to retreat from danger. (1986, pp 12-13)

Hence 'egalitarian grounds' do not apply; if they did, then police would not be obliged to tackle armed people. The authors' dismissal of this argument on the grounds that the state does not discharge its obligations to 'threatened minorities' and others is specious even if the factual claim is accepted. The state *explicitly* imposes upon police officers certain duties which expose them to danger, whereas even if it disregards entirely - even as a matter of policy - racial violence, it places no duty on those who suffer such violence to expose themselves to this danger. In any case, even if it is true that the state discharges its responsibilities to the police more adequately than it does for other citizens, such a failure does not excuse it from discharging its duty as completely as possible.

Nevertheless, it remains true that arming the police may displace the risk from them to innocent persons killed and injured accidentally. However, even this argument is not nearly as simple as Jacobs and Sanders make it sound, for refusing to arm the police might *also* expose *innocent third parties* to danger. For example, unarmed police would be impotent in preventing armed terrorists from siaughtering passengers in an airport terminal. Thus, the danger is not simply transferred from the police to other citizens, but from the police *and* one group of innocent citizens to other innocent citizens. Of course much the same applies to the ambulance and fire services, for in speeding to convey someone

- 74 -

to hospital or extinguish a fire they too expose other citizens to the risk of accidental death or injury. Perhaps this is what the authors have in mind when they make an exception 'where the safety of the general public would otherwise be jeopardised' (Jacobs and Sanders 1986, p 13). Yet, once this point is conceded, the absolute refusal to allow police to carry firearms is renounced, to be replaced by the question of how many firearms should be issued under what circumstances. As has been shown above, the police have pursued and are continuing to pursue a cautious policy in this regard.

Conclusions

Whilst ultimately unconvincing, the Jacobs and Sanders (1986) argument clearly draws our attention to the considerable responsibility that accompanies the arming of police. Policy in Britain has been conservative: the arming of police was precipitated by the growth in armed crime and terrorism, systematic training was only begun once it became clear that it could no longer be avoided, and the intention is to maintain only small teams of highly-trained specialised officers for armed operations. On the other hand, it must be said that whilst caution in this area of policy-making is generally to be commended, it seems that it has been adopted by default. Developments have been forced upon policy-makers by events. The Home Office Working Party Report (Home Office 1986a), though in many ways a sensible document, gives little indication that the problems of dealing with armed operations have fully been appreciated. One hopes that it will not require another disaster to promote still further developments in training and operational arrangements.

CHAPTER SIX

'DEADLY FORCE'

Introduction

To some extent the fears expressed in the past by senior
police officers - namely, that to acknowledge openly that
police do carry firearms, albeit occasionally, would promote
public concern - have proven well-founded. Controversial
incidents, especially tragic mistaken and accidental shootings
have not only raised issues of selection, training and
supervision, but also anxieties about an aggressive style of
policing. Thus, after the shooting of Mrs. Groce, a speaker at
the Labour Party Conference asked rhetorically, 'Why all these
guns?'. Nor does it need an accident or mistake to spark such
a response. For example, following the incident at the Sir
John Soane's Museum on 6 February 1987 when two armed robbers
burst in at closing time to be met by armed police who opened
fire when one of the robbers continued brandishing his gun
despite warnings and was shot dead, Mr. Frank Dobson, Labour
MP for Holborn was reported as saying: 'I am shocked. We need
an immediate independent inquiry. Police are loafing around
with guns far too much'. A policy adviser to the Association
of London Authorities remarked: 'Arming gun-crazy cops and
telling them to shoot on sight is no solution in a democratic
society' (*Sunday Mirror* 8 February 1987).

Indeed, the mere appearance of officers carrying the Heckler
and Koch MP5 machine guns at Heathrow Airport provoked
considerable controversy. Nor is this controversy limited to
critics of the police. When the Police Federation's magazine
Police contained a cover photograph of divisional riflemen
posing with their rifles it prompted a police officer to

write:

> I cannot help saying in the first instance, after 30
> years public service, how disappointed and dejected I
> feel.

> This is not what the public wants to see and indeed, not
> what the public should see, although I accept the
> necessity, from time to time, to be prepared for such
> armed conflicts. All you have done is display our
> organisation in such an abhorrent 'macho' image, that
> such weaponry would only be matched by counter-weaponry.

What seems to concern people is that having abandoned the
cautious 'amateurism' of the previous era, the British police
seem now to have adopted the aggressive approach more commonly
associated with American and Continental styles of policing.
Therefore we need to consider whether tactics are
unwarrantably aggressive and whether the weapons used are more
lethal than they need be.

"Shoot to Kill"?

Perhaps one of the most serious worries is that armed officers
are taught to 'shoot to kill'. This concern seems to underlie
such casual remarks as that made by Mr. Tony Banks, MP,
following the Sir John Soane's Museum shooting: 'Too often
police are shooting first and questioning later' (*People*, 8
February 1987). These anxieties have been most fully and
forcefully articulated by Sarah Manwaring-White (1983) who,
after an apparently thorough review of police weaponry and
tactics, concludes :

> ...it is obvious that an increasing number of officers
> are being trained to shoot to kill and more are trained
> every year. They are told to aim at the chest area and to
> do whatever is necessary to protect their colleagues and
> the public . . . Training has become a matter of course
> and 'shoot to kill' has replaced the old instruction of

using a gun as the last resort in self defence. (1983, p 130-32)

This allegation is given apparent credence by quoting the injudicious remarks of two Chief Constables: Mr. John Alderson, then Chief Constable of Devon and Cornwall, who is reported as saying 'We are prepared to shoot to kill in the interests of society if necessary', and Mr. John Duke, Chief Constable of Hampshire, who is quoted as saying, 'The gun is not made for protection, nor made to injure or to frighten. It is made to kill, and police officers being trained to use it when necessary in Hampshire are being trained with this in mind' (Manwaring-White, 1983, p 117). More recently the Parliamentary Adviser to the Police Federation, Sir Eldon Griffiths MP, was quoted as saying that the police 'always shoot to kill' and do so as a matter of duty (Sun 10 July 1987).

In fact, Manwaring-White's case is flimsy and ill-informed. Let us consider the points made in reverse order. Perhaps the statements made by the two Chief Constables were ill-advised and made without consideration of how they might later be used by critics such as Manwaring-White. Yet, even as they stand, they do not offer support for Manwaring-White's extravagant conclusions. Alderson is saying no more than is and always has been the truth, for as 'monopolists of force in civil society' (Bittner, 1974) the police must be prepared ultimately to use lethal force to fulfil their mandate of protecting the public. Thus, if it is necessary to shoot and kill a terrorist machine-gunning passengers in an airport lounge, this will be the duty of the police. This is not a revolutionary change: the police used firearms to engage anarchistic terrorists at the 'Siege of Sidney Street'. What has changed is the scale of preparedness made necessary by the growth in armed crime and terrorism.

Mr. Duke too is uttering no more than a truism. A gun is not designed to fend off bullets, but is only effective when fired, and when it is fired at someone is likely to prove fatal. When he says that Hampshire police officers are trained with this in mind he is doing no more than repeat the generally accepted guidance on police use of firearms.

Metropolitan Police policy, as taught to all AFOs, is quite explicit on this:

> An authorised firearms officer is trained to shoot at a given area – usually the torso. Any shot aimed at that target area is likely to result in grievous bodily harm being caused. Therefore, if an officer shoots with the intention not to kill the suspect, but to stop him, he must realise that a possible consequence is the death of the suspect. He must therefore believe before he shoots that causing grievous bodily harm or possibly killing the suspect is reasonable under those particular circumstances and that the conditions of Section 3 Criminal Law Act 1967 apply.

> It follows that if the circumstances would not justify the killing there must be no attempt to stop a suspect by shooting merely to wound him.

There are, then, two related but separable points to be considered. The first is that the *purpose* of shooting someone is not to kill them, but to stop them committing some extreme act. The goal is not death, but total and immediate incapacitation. The second point is that the *consequence* of shooting someone is probably, though not inevitably, that they will be killed. The policy is cautious, rather than cavalier in the manner suggested by Manwaring-White, because it insists that police can open fire only when they would be justified in killing the person *even if death does not result*. In contrast to the impression conveyed by Manwaring-White, the policy is conservative, for it insists that firearms be used only as a last resort in the most extreme circumstances.

The reference made by Duke to using guns to 'frighten' people also leads, in fact, to the opposite conclusion to that arrived at by Manwaring-White. Two of the six safety rules which AFOs must learn by rote and be prepared to recite whenever challenged, state, 'Never draw your weapon from the holster unless you have occasion to use it' and 'Never point a firearm at anyone unless you are prepared to shoot'. In other words, officers are specifically warned *not* to draw their weapons and point them simply in order to intimidate someone.

Drawing a gun from the holster is a serious matter, which must be reported to senior officers, and is not to be undertaken lightly.

If the purpose of shooting at suspects is to stop rather than kill them, why is it necessary to fire twice in 'sense of direction' shooting? This question was implicitly raised by an editorial in the *Morning Star* newspaper following the fatal shooting of an armed robber at the Sir John Soane's Museum on the 6 February 1987 (*Morning Star* 9 February 1987). It demanded a 'satisfactory answer' to the question why 'a man was shot twice', implying that this was somehow improper. There is an answer: police are trained to fire two shots in rapid succession when firing 'sense of direction' because these shots are fired at close range when immediate incapacitation is absolutely essential given the imminence of the threat. In view of the urgency of the situation and the lack of time in which to take aim, one shot might miss the armed person and in the time it would take to appreciate this the suspect could have fired and killed the officer. Moreover, if only one bullet struck the person there is no guarantee that it would totally incapacitate and prevent the suspect returning fire. In fact, the shooting at the Sir John Soane's Museum provides a good illustration of the difficulties that can arise in such circumstances. One of the bullets fired at Denis Bergin actually struck the butt of the shotgun he was carrying. Only one bullet actually struck his body. The other man who was shot was hit by a single bullet in the arm. In the confined space of the hallway of the museum, a failure totally to incapacitate an armed person could easily prove fatal to the police or other innocent people.

If the police must only open fire when justified in using lethal force, should they not wait until their adversaries open fire upon them? In other words, are the police 'shooting first and questioning later' as Tony Banks MP suggests? (*People*, 8 February 1987) This was one of the many issues raised during the course of the trial of Inspector Douglas Lovelock, who was charged with the malicious wounding of Mrs. Groce. It was reported that Inspector Lovelock said in evidence that he would only fire if fired upon (*The Times* 10 January 1987). Moreover, prosecuting counsel claimed that since the second of the two safety rules cited above previously included the phrase 'unless you *intend* to use it', then Lovelock could not claim that he had fired the gun at Mrs. Groce unintentionally. More recently the *Guardian* newspaper, comparing the shootings at the Sir John Soane's Museum and the abattoir at Plumstead, remarked:

> In both cases, police had staked out a robbery target. In both cases, the robbers were armed. In both cases, so far as is known, police procedures were followed. But, in both cases too, it was only the police who fired, not the robbers.

The editorial concluded:

> It does look as though ... the police are more prepared to carry the fight to the criminals than they used to be. It may not actually be a shoot-to-kill policy - such a thing would be illegal - but it may look like one to the professional armed robbers.

If officers were to be constrained only to draw their own weapon when confronted by a person who also had a weapon drawn, or only to point it at another when intending to shoot, or to fire only when fired upon, then this would be tantamount to inviting them to commit suicide. To draw a weapon from the holster, especially when that weapon is concealed under a tunic or jacket, would take much too long. A person armed with, say, a shotgun, would have ample time to aim and fire before the police officer's weapon had cleared the holster. Only to point a gun when an officer intends to fire it, would again expose an officer to undue risk from a sudden attack. To fire only when fired upon is a prescription for certain death, because if hit by 'SG' shotgun pellets the officer would, in all probability, be dead before he could return fire. Thus, officers must be allowed to draw their gun from the holster when they reasonably apprehend that there is an armed threat. Similarly, it is essential that officers should fire their weapon when they reasonably anticipate that an armed person is about to open fire.

The extent of the danger to which armed officers are exposed when confronting armed suspects is illustrated by the fate of one such policeman, PC Bishop of the Essex Police. In 1984 he and other officers staged a carefully planned interception of an armed robber at the seaside town of Frimley. When the man arrived at the scene of the interception he was challenged by Bishop whose gun was drawn and pointing at him. Nevertheless, the gunman was able to fire both barrels of his sawn-off shotgun from within a bag that he was carrying. The shot killed Bishop and seriously wounded his colleague standing near to him. A shot fired by a third officer armed with a shotgun gravely wounded the gunman, but was not quick enough to save Bishop and his colleague. Although having his gun drawn did not save Bishop, to require officers in similar circumstances to keep their weapon holstered would increase the risk to them significantly. Similarly, when members of the Metropolitan Police Force Firearms Unit confronted suspected armed robbers in Woolwich in November 1987, the Inspector leading the team, Dwight Atkinson, was shot in the leg as he called out a warning.

The fate of PC Bishop and his colleague, and Inspector Atkinson puts other, more controversial, incidents into proper perspective. For example, the killing of Michael Calvey in 1978 has been criticised because he was hit in the back during a raid on a supermarket in Eltham by a shot fired by officers lying in wait. The pathologist explained at the inquest that the wound indicated that Calvey had been in the act of turning towards the officer when hit. A fully loaded double-barrelled shotgun was in his possession at the time and was recovered from the scene. Had the officer not fired when he did, allowing Calvey to aim the shotgun towards him, he might well have suffered the same fate as Bishop. An even more striking parallel with the murder of Bishop was the shooting by police of two robbers at a North London sub-post office in 1984. When challenged, one of the robbers reached into a holdall he was carrying. Fearing that it concealed a shotgun, the officers opened fire wounding the man and his accomplice. Upon inspection the bag was found not to contain a weapon. Of course, the officers could not have known that at the time and had it done so they too might have been killed as Bishop was later to be killed. Inevitably, armed officers may be called upon to make a split-second decision which might, with hindsight, prove to have been made in error. An erroneous decision to open fire might lead to the injury or death of an innocent person, the opposite error may result in the death or injury of the officer himself.

Of course, the police cannot be licenced to fire upon suspects no matter what the circumstances, nor does the law allow them to do so. They can only use such force as is 'reasonable in the circumstances'. However, when it comes to judging what is 'reasonable in the circumstances', the actual hazards of armed operations must be kept in mind. The possession of a gun does not make a police officer invulnerable and he must make split-second decisions upon which his life and the lives of others might depend. This undoubtedly creates a recurring dilemma, not least for the officer holding the gun, but it is not a dilemma that can be eliminated by imposing such restrictions on police officers that would repeatedly place their lives in jeopardy.

A third point raised by the quote from Mr. Duke regards so-called 'shooting to kill' as opposed to 'shooting to wound'. As he remarks, guns are designed to kill not merely to injure and the official guidelines explicitly forbid officers from attempting to stop a suspect by shooting to wound him. Why not shoot simply to wound or to knock a weapon from a person's hand? Although it sometimes happens that people shot by the police receive wounds to their arm or leg, it would be unsafe to instruct officers to aim at these parts of the body. First, limbs are the most mobile parts of the body and, therefore, most difficult to hit. Second, they make relatively small targets. Thus, it is far easier to miss a limb than it is to miss the torso which is larger and less mobile. A bullet, even a relatively short range revolver or pistol bullet, will travel some considerable distance beyond the person it has missed and may, in consequence, endanger innocent people. Whilst it is true that many people who are shot by police do not die (Milton *et al* 1977) it would be hazardous for police to shoot on the assumption that their bullets will prove less than lethal. A bullet may strike a bone or item of jewellery or property in a pocket and be deflected, with the result that a perfectly aimed shot designed to wound could still prove fatal. Third, shots which hit the limbs almost invariably 'over penetrate', that is, they exit from the body after only being slowed a little, thereby causing a hazard to innocent bystanders. Shooting a gun out of another person's hand is, of course, fantasy reserved for screen heroes.

Moreover, as Greenwood (1979) points out, if police were permitted to 'shoot to wound' they may actually kill more people, for this might lower the threshold at which an armed officer might be tempted to fire his gun. Instead of allowing an escaping suspect to get away, an officer may fire at him in order simply to effect an arrest. Given the possibilities for error, there would be a distinct chance that such a shot would actually prove lethal and more people would be killed. Thus, it is in the public interest that the threshold for the use of deadly force be maintained at the highest possible level - deadly force should only be used in deadly earnest.

Thus, police policy is in this respect conservative: it insists that only where an officer would be justified in using lethal force can he open fire. It is for these reasons that the training manual forbids shots aimed to wound the person and also states: 'Warning shots will not be fired by police'. This is because a shot that does not hit its target may hit another person unintentionally.

If police policy was genuinely designed to kill rather than simply to stop a suspect (as Manwaring-White maintains), it could be achieved more simply and directly by the expedient of aiming for the head. Although smaller than the torso and quite mobile, the head presents a reasonable target, especially at close quarters. Shots to the head are more likely to prove lethal. Again, head shots by snipers could easily be justified as totally incapacitating the person since destroying the brain stem would prevent him from even reacting to being shot by squeezing a trigger or detonating an explosive charge. Yet the police instruct officers to aim at the torso and on practice targets the head is not included in the zone which receives highest marks. Thus, the policy, in this connection as in others, is not to 'shoot to kill' but to inflict minimum necessary injury even at the cost of reducing rapid and effective incapacitation. Whether this is the correct policy will be discussed later.

Man-Stopping Bullets

This brings us to the question of the weaponry issued to police, particularly the type of ammunition used and whether it is gratuitously injurious. Benn and Worpole make the extraordinary claim that the Smith and Wesson is :

> a large calibre revolver originally developed for hunting in the US and known there as the "grizzly-bear killer". No other European countries issue their police with such large hand guns, guns which it seems lack the double-safety devices of other pistols. (1986, p 64)

Others have noted that some officers are issued with Smith and Wesson model 19s and 28s, or what they refer to as the 'Magnum .357"' and conclude that this is an unwarrantably powerful weapon for police use in Britain (Rusbridger 1985).

These comments reveal two areas of confusion: that between the revolver and the propellant power of the ammunition fired, and between revolvers and self-loading pistols. This section will examine the first source of confusion and the next will consider the second.

Contrary to the impression conveyed by television and cinema portrayals of armed police, there is no such weapon as the 'Magnum'. Thus, when Clint Eastwood says, in the soliloquy from 'Dirty Harry', 'This is a Magnum 44, the most powerful handgun in the world ... so all you've got to ask yourself is "Do I feel lucky today?"', he is talking nonsense. The term 'Magnum' refers not to the gun, but to the propellant power of the round fired by the gun. In fact, just to confuse matters, the .357" Magnum round is the same diameter as the .38" round (the difference in nomenclature being due to where on the cartridge the measurement is taken). The difference between these rounds is the power of the propellant and the length of the cartridge case which accommodates it. In fact, there are a variety of .38" rounds which differ in their power and, thus, their muzzle velocity. The .380", or '.38" short' as it is sometimes known, is the least powerful; the .38" standard is next most powerful; that is followed by the .38" special and the .38" special + p; and finally the .357" Magnum is the most powerful. The round that is currently approved by the Home Office for issue to the police is the .38" special + p 125 grain bullet, about which more will be written later.

Confusion arises because not all .38" rounds can be fired from the same gun. As the power of the round increases so too does the length of the cartridge case. This is partly necessitated by the need to accommodate the propellant itself, but also ensures that weapons which are not designed to withstand greater pressures cannot fire the more powerful cartridges. Thus, a .357" Magnum round would fit into the chamber of a Smith and Wesson model 10, but it would protrude beyond the length of the chamber, thus preventing the cylinder from being closed and the bullet fired. However, any of the various .38" rounds could be fired from a model 19 or model 28 which are issued to instructors, because the length of the cartridge would be less than that of the chamber.

Why issue revolvers capable of firing the Magnum round, if this round is not actually used? Any gun designed to fire a Magnum round tends to be more robust than its counterparts designed to fire less powerful ammunition, because this round when fired imposes greater stress upon the weapon. Thus, an additional advantage of supplying model 19s and 28s to instructors who use them quite frequently in training and instruction, is that they are more durable. Moreover, heavier weapons tend to be more accurate. In short, the fact that some officers may be equipped with revolvers capable of firing more powerful ammunition, does not mean that they will actually fire the most powerful ammunition the gun is capable of chambering.

Thus, to say that the Smith and Wesson is a 'large calibre revolver' (Benn and Worpole 1986, p 64) is simply to confuse the weapon and the power of the ammunition. It may be conceivable that a .357" Magnum round could kill a grizzly-bear, but a .380" almost certainly would not. By the same token to compare the Smith and Wesson .38" revolver with the 9mm self-loading pistols typically issued to Continental police forces is misleading. In fact, the 9mm round is almost exactly the same diameter as the .38" round. Moreover, just as .38" ammunition has its more or less powerful variants, so too does 9mm ammunition.

That said, it must also be acknowledged that there has been a drift towards the use of more powerful ammunition over the years. The 158 grain .38" special replaced the .380" and more recently it in turn has been replaced by the 125 grain .38" special + p round. The decision to change from the .380" to the .38" special was dictated by problems in the supply of ammunition, which is governed to a large extent by the large American market. The switch from the 158 grain .38" special to the 125 grain .38" special + p was made in order to provide the police with ammunition which had greater stopping power. However, it is a type of round which in 1973 was refused to the Metropolitan Police (Gould and Waldren 1986, p 202) and was described by the *Daily Telegraph* as being 'softer and flat nosed so as to spread on impact' (quoted in Gould and Waldren 1986, p 201).

Hence, there may appear to be some substance in claims that the police are using more powerful ammunition than they need and which, from the *Daily Telegraph's* description, appears to be a form of 'dum-dum' bullet outlawed by international treaty. Indeed the decision to adopt semi-jacketed semi-wadcutter ammunition was taken in the knowledge that it departed from the strict letter of the Hague Conventions of 1889, 1899 and 1907 the provisions of which British and European governments have extended unilaterally to the police. These Conventions stipulate that military ammunition must be fully-jacketed round-nosed and not designed to disintegrate or explode upon impact. It explicitly forbids 'hollow-point' bullets, commonly referred to as 'dum-dum' bullets. However, these Conventions have never applied to policing: restrictions on police ammunition have been a unilateral extension of the provisions of the Conventions by government.

The choice of a semi-wadcutter semi-jacketed round departs from the Hague Convention insofar as the bullet is not fully-jacketed and might, therefore, be seen as gratuitously lethal. In fact, the 125 grain revolver bullet and its 95 grain parabellum equivalent were chosen from a range of alternatives because they gave necessary stopping power with *least* injury. This calls for some clarification of the notion of 'stopping power' - a discussion which for the moment will be restricted to low velocity bullets like those fired from revolvers. Bullets are not effective simply because they create a hole through the body. The sheer impact of the bullet will cause a degree of injury (as can be seen from the 'trauma' inflicted upon wearers of light-weight body armour), but this, by itself, will not cause a person to be knocked down, for the impact will be no greater than the recoil felt by the person firing the gun. The effectiveness of a bullet depends on the transfer of its kinetic energy to the bodily tissue of the person hit. Hence the desirability that the bullet should come to rest within the body of the person aimed at, depositing all its energy, and not over-penetrate. The effectiveness with which kinetic energy is transferred is affected by a variety of factors including the velocity, size, weight and shape of the bullet. These will determine the size and shape of the cavity created in the flesh by the bullet's sudden de-acceleration. It is this cavity which causes injury with associated shock and the possibility that some vital organ will be hit. Even then it is not inevitable that a person who is hit will be immediately and totally incapacitated. It is now appreciated that people in a state of high arousal secrete chemicals, known as 'endorphins', which act as pain-killers and reduce their vulnerability to injury. Also, a person under the influence of drugs can be relatively immune to the immediate traumatic impact of bullets.

Thus, the dilemma in selecting ammunition for police use, is to choose a round which will inflict sufficient injury as to have a reasonable likelihood of stopping the person from doing whatever justified shooting him in the first instance, whilst not inflicting more injury than is necessary. The 158 grain fully-jacketed bullet, with which the police were previously equipped, lacked stopping power because it, like all fully-jacketed round-nose bullets, tends to over-penetrate and hence fails to deposit all its energy within the person aimed at. Experimental tests conducted on behalf of the Home Office also questioned the ability of any of the ammunition tested to retain its integrity upon striking bone. There was a tendency for the brass jacket of fully-jacketed rounds to become detached from the lead bullet. In itself, this could be seen as arguably contravening the Hague Conventions which forbid bullets which disintegrate upon impact. Some other rounds overcome this tendency but do so only at the cost of inflicting serious injuries. The French made THV round is hollow (but note *not* hollow-point) and fully-jacketed, and gives up its energy very freely upon impact. However, it causes an enormous entry wound which the Home Office regards as unacceptable. Thus, if the police had truly adopted a policy of 'shooting to kill', they could have adopted far more lethal ammunition which could more easily have been justified as being consistent with the Hague Conventions than that which has actually been adopted.

Conformity with the stipulations of the Hague Conventions hitherto and the continued reluctance to depart from them testify to the conservative minimalist approach of the British authorities over the years. But the questions must be asked: Is policy on ammunition *too* conservative and minimalist? As noted above, police officers are instructed to fire two shots in rapid succession when firing by 'sense of direction' in order totally to incapacitate an armed antagonist. Initial press reports of the Plumstead Abattoir shooting in July 1987 clearly indicates that when paired shots strike a person they do indeed incapacitate effectively. That shooting also demonstrated that where only a single shot hits a person they are *not* necessarily incapacitated and might retain hold of their weapon. This replicated the experience of the shooting at the Sir John Soane's Museum, where one of the raiders was shot in the arm but was able to escape from the scene before being arrested by pursuing officers. Therefore, there is no guarantee that an armed person struck by a single shot will not be able to return fire, shoot innocent third parties or detonate explosives. *There would appear to be prima facie grounds for suggesting that much more powerful ammunition should be supplied to armed officers so that the need to fire twice becomes less necessary.*

The kind of ammunition which would possess sufficient stopping power would undoubtedly be more lethal. The .357" Magnum hollow-point has been adopted by many American police forces as the round which achieves a satisfactory compromise between effective stopping power and minimal injury. The additional propellant power of the Magnum cartridge is needed to produce the expansion of the bullet upon impact which causes the injury which incapacitates. It is unlikely that many people shot with such a bullet would survive, but lethality does not simply equate with stopping power. The robber shot by PC Sliman in 1972 subsequently died, but was not immediately incapacitated by the .380" bullet that struck him. On the other hand, those who have been hit by *both* the paired shots using the semi-jacketed semi-wadcutter bullets have died. The use of a more powerful round would not seriously increase the lethal consequences of being shot by the police, but it would increase the likelihood of immediate and total incapacitation.

Almost any ammunition which achieved sufficient stopping-power is likely to breach the Hague Conventions, but are the standards imposed by the Hague Conventions appropriate or prudent when applied to police work? After all, armed criminals and terrorists are not party to the Conventions which apply only to the military forces of signatory states during times of war. Moreover, the fully-jacketed round stipulated by the Conventions tends to over-penetrate and ricochet, thus proving less effective and more dangerous to innocent bystanders than alternative rounds which the Conventions forbid. These are important considerations relating to *any* police ammunition, but are of particular significance in regard to close protection officers who are armed with .38" special + p ammunition and riflemen who are currently issued with 7.62mm or .223" fully-jacketed ball ammunition of military design.

Protection officers, for whom the most serious threat is an assassination attempt made at close quarters by someone in a crowd, need ammunition which will utterly incapacitate a possibly drugged or crazed assassin with minimal risk of over-penetration. Greenwood argues that for this role it is 'irresponsible' to use anything other than hollow-point ammunition (1979, p 296), whilst Yardley and Eliot (1986c) prefer the recently developed 'Glaser safety slug', a fully-jacketed round which contains a number of small pellets which are liberated within the body of a person shot once the outer casing strikes him causing enormous injuries and rejected by the Home Office for this reason. Either of these rounds are more likely to incapacitate even a determined attacker with little risk of over-penetration or ricochets than is currently issued ammunition. However, despite these purely technical advantages, the Home Office has rejected the use of this kind of ammunition because it would inflict injuries which are considered to be ethically unjustifiable and inconsistent with the Hague Conventions.

Achieving a balance between technical suitability and ethical acceptability is even more difficult in the case of high-velocity rifle ammunition. The police are currently permitted to use only ball ammunition of military design which strictly complies with the provisions of the Hague Conventions. However, high velocity ammunition of this kind is almost invariably lethal, because once the muzzle velocity of a bullet exceeds 2,000 feet per second (and the 7.62mm Enforcer bullet has a muzzle velocity of 3,000 feet per second) it causes a particular kind of injury to the person. As it passes through the body the bullet creates a tremendous shock wave ahead of, and all around, its path. This causes the large exit wounds and enormous injuries for which these weapons have become notorious. Not only is the injury from such a weapon almost invariably fatal, but the bullet is almost certain to over-penetrate and moving with such velocity could hit others with devastating consequences. This is illustrated by the injuries caused to Governor Connelly who was wounded during the assassination of President Kennedy in Dallas in 1963. One of the bullets which is thought to have struck the President in the back of the neck, is then believed to have exited through the front of the throat and hit Connelly who was seated in front of Kennedy in the same car. The bullet hit Connelly in the back and then exited from his chest and struck him in the wrist and eventually came to rest in his thigh upon which his hand was resting. Fortunately, Connelly survived, but this was his good fortune, others might not be so lucky. A bullet which missed its target could continue uninterrupted for up to two miles and is also capable of passing through substantial obstacles whilst retaining enough energy to kill. Moreover the path of such a bullet could not be predicted if it was to ricochet.

High velocity weapons are necessary for riflemen because used at long distance, they must retain their accuracy. However, the problems of over-penetration and ricochets could be mitigated, if not solved, by the adoption of some kind of soft-nosed bullet. These rounds would cause horrendous injuries to anyone they struck, and would almost certainly prove fatal. However, the high-velocity ball ammunition now issued to riflemen is hardly less lethal. Unlike ball ammunition, soft-nosed rounds will not penetrate obstacles such as walls, nor do they ricochet so easily, because they tend to disintegrate upon impact. It seems that the desire not to be seen to adopt a type of ammunition most injurious to the suspect has overruled concern for the safety of innocent people who might suffer the fate of Governor Connelly, or worse.

The Safety of Weapons

The second issue raised by Benn and Worpole is the safety of guns 'which it seems lack the double-safety devices of other pistols' (1986, p 64). They are not alone in voicing such concern. The issue arose most pointedly during the trials of PC Chester and Inspector Lovelock. The defence to each of the charges these officers faced was in essence the same, that the gun was accidentally discharged by a startled officer. This, not unnaturally, led to questions about the safety of the revolvers issued to these officers and anxiety that they seemed to lack 'safety catches'.

In fact, revolvers are not fitted with 'safety catches', they are a feature of self-loading pistols that will be dealt with in detail later. The safety of a revolver relies upon its firing mechanism, for a revolver fired in 'double-action' is an inherently safe weapon. This calls for some explanation of 'double' versus 'single-action' shooting. Double-action means that when the revolver's hammer is in the closed position and then the trigger is depressed the cylinder rotates and the hammer is forced back until it drops forward under the pressure of a spring onto the firing pin causing the round in the chamber to be fired. This requires between ten and thirteen pounds of pressure on the trigger of the Smith and Wesson model 10 and the trigger must travel some considerable distance in order to operate the mechanism. This makes double-action shooting an inherently safe procedure. Single-action, on the other hand, means that in the case of a revolver the hammer is manually retracted until it locks (sometimes called 'cocking' the hammer), which in consequence rotates the cylinder, positioning the next round in line with the barrel. Then the merest touch on the trigger (three pounds in the case of the model 10) releases the hammer which fires the round. The advantage of this mode of shooting is that the reduced pressure upon, and shorter distance travelled by, the trigger allows greater accuracy. For that reason single-action is favoured by competition marksmen. However, it is obviously much less safe, since inadvertent pressure on the trigger would be sufficient to fire a round accidentally.

Until the report of the Home Office Working Party (1986a), Metropolitan Police officers were instructed in how to fire the revolver in both 'single' and 'double-action'. This was justified as necessary because it was a feature of the weapon and it was important for officers to know how it operated. It was also thought to have some operational value for carefully aimed shooting at long distances and accuracy at 25 metres is undoubtedly improved when firing single-action. However, the evident dangers inherent in this procedure convinced the Home Office Working Party that this mode of firing the weapon was too dangerous to be continued (Home Office, 1986a). There have been suggestions that under stress officers might place the gun in single-action without realizing they have done so and certainly the news film of the Oldham incident (referred to on p 33) shows a supposedly trained AFO doing precisely this and then pushing the gun, still in single-action, into his pocket!

The situation now is that AFOs are familiarised with 'single-action' shooting, but are instructed never to use it operationally and are not required to qualify either initially or on refresher courses in this mode of shooting. The justification for continuing to familiarise officers with 'single-action' is that they need to be apprised of its dangers and to be aware that this is a capability of the weapon, knowledge of which they may need should they be required to make safe a revolver found with its hammer 'cocked'. What is not clear is why police revolvers continue to retain the facility for firing in 'single-action'. Some American police forces have adapted the internal mechanism of their revolvers to prevent this mode of firing and the simple expedient of removing the hammer-spur would make it extremely difficult to 'cock' the hammer. The fact that the Metropolitan Police have not taken such action and relied on a simple proscription seems to reveal a touching faith in the efficacy of rules and the influence they might have over officers in a tense and possibly frightening situation. Surely, if single-action shooting is inherently dangerous, then the means of doing it should be removed.

Safe Handling

The safety of weapons is not guaranteed by safety catches or other mechanical features which can be disengaged. The way in which a weapon is handled is much more important for ensuring that it is safe. As the trials of PC Chester of the West Midlands Police and Inspector Lovelock of the Metropolitan Police both illustrate, there is the danger that innocent people might be accidentally shot as a result of an armed officer being startled. For example, Inspector Lovelock explained how he tensed, causing the gun to fire, as a shape loomed out of the darkness.

The likelihood that such an accident will occur is increased by the stance adopted by armed officers. The so-called 'isosceles' stance involves holding the butt of the gun with both hands, arms pushed forward and locked at the elbow, with the knees flexed. The reason for locking the elbows is that under extreme stress muscular control can be diminished, especially in the limbs, causing the condition known colloquially by some American police as the 'liquorice arm'. Massad Ayoob, whose system of gunfighting is founded on the need to overcome stress, insists that the isosceles position is the most robust stance yet devised (Ayoob 1984). Unfortunately, since the upper body is locked when adopting this stance, the muscles of the trigger finger are amongst the few parts of anatomy that are left free to contract if the officer is startled.

This danger is reduced by the practice of never fingering the trigger until the last possible moment - even a drawn weapon is held with the finger resting outside the trigger guard. In the event of the officer being startled the trigger could not be inadvertently squeezed. However, there are difficulties concerning this practice, for normally, the finger rests along the frame of the gun in the outstretched position and, if it becomes necessary to finger the trigger, it is simultaneously repositioned and bent around the trigger. Unfortunately, the weakness in this practice, is that under stress there is a tendency to exaggerate the contraction of the finger muscles as the finger wraps around the trigger, thus making an accidental discharge likely. Ayoob recommends that even when resting outside the trigger guard, the finger should always be kept bent so that no further muscular contraction is required when fingering the trigger; all that is necessary is that the finger is repositioned and the likelihood of accidental discharge is minimised. This seems to be a sensible recommendation which should be incorporated into training.

Revolvers versus Self-loading Pistols

Despite the inherent safety of revolvers critics have drawn invidious comparisons between this type of weapon and the self-loading pistols that Continental police tend to use (Benn and Worpole 1986, Rusbridger 1985). However, not all Metropolitan Police officers rely upon revolvers: selected officers are issued with the Browning self-loading pistol which, as mentioned above, offers greater firepower than the model 10 revolver, having 13 rounds in the magazine. Within the police itself the weapon is popular with those trained to use it and there is pressure from other departments for their officers also to be issued with the Browning. It might seem that we are faced with the quite unusual situation of, at least some, police and their critics agreeing upon the suitability of weaponry. Unfortunately, there are reasons to question the Browning's, or any other self-loading pistol's, suitability as a police weapon.

It is important to recognise the important differences between this type of weapon and the revolver. In a revolver, each round is placed into its individual chamber and as the gun is fired the cylinder revolves bringing each chamber into line with the barrel and firing-pin in succession. The round itself, once positioned in the chamber does not move. By contrast, the rounds in a self-loading pistol are taken out of the magazine and pushed into the breech very rapidly. This is a complex and forceful mechanical process which is more likely to result in the weapon jamming because the round is not properly seated in the breech. Jamming may also occur if a bullet misfires and does not create sufficient pressure to operate the mechanism. When this occurs the slide has to be retracted manually, to eject the jammed round. Sometimes the round can be so badly jammed that the gun has to be disassembled to clear it. When a jam does occur the weapon is incapable of firing any more shots until the jam is cleared. The Walther PP (a standard Continental police pistol) carried by Inspector Beeton when acting as Princess Anne's bodyguard was of this design and jammed after he had fired one shot at the man attempting to assassinate/abduct her. Once this occurred, and having been wounded, he was virtually powerless to protect the Princess (Rae 1987). Revolvers, on the other hand, are mechanically much simpler and, therefore, there is less likelihood that things can go wrong. If they do go wrong and the round does not fire for some reason, then all that is needed is for the handler to squeeze the trigger once again, thus revolving the cylinder and bringing another round into position and firing it.

The sheer mechanical complexity of the self-loading pistol, which demands a very high standard of handling skill, makes this a weapon of limited use for police officers who may have to use the weapon in an emergency. Even in the safety of the practice range the complexities of handling the gun cause difficulties. For example, during range practice either weapon is usually fired until it is empty and then has to be made safe, 'proved' (that is, shown to be unloaded) and returned to the holster. In the case of a revolver this simply involves opening the cylinder and ejecting all the spent cartridge cases so that the empty chambers are exposed for inspection. The Browning, on the other hand, completes its final firing sequence with the slide held back automatically. The magazine must then be removed, the slide-release catch depressed causing the slide to spring forward, the empty magazine inserted once again and the hammer manually lowered whilst the trigger is depressed, and finally the magazine removed. One can see from comparing these range procedures for the two types of weapon that the Browning is far more complex than a revolver. This complexity could be, indeed has been, crucial in a real gunfight, particularly if the weapon jammed and had to be cleared.

A further problem arises from the complexity of the firing mechanism and this is the need for the user to adopt a sound firing position. Unless the arms are locked so that the recoil from the gun can be fully absorbed by the user the energy from the recoil can be dissipated. This can result in the slide mechanism failing to work adequately and the gun jamming. Such a firing position is taught to users of both self-loading pistols *and* revolvers, but in an actual gunfight an officer acting under stress or possibly injured might not be able to adopt an ideal firing position. For example, in 1972 PC Peter Sliman shot and mortally wounded an armed robber *after* he himself had been shot and was lying on the pavement. It is highly improbable to suppose that he achieved this feat by adopting the prescribed firing position. Had he not been using a revolver, with its simple mechanism, it is less likely that he would have been able effectively to return fire.

Yet another problem arising from the complexity of the mechanism is the restrictions it places on the type of ammunition used. Because the round has to be transferred from the magazine to the breech before being fired, the gun is designed to fire fully-jacketed round-nosed bullets. A fully-jacketed bullet has the lead bullet encased in a steel, copper, nickel or brass sleeve or coat. This enables it to resist any distortion as it is wrenched from the magazine and slammed into the breech. Travel from magazine to the breech is aided by a round-nosed bullet shape which most readily slides up the ramp and into position. Unfortunately, as noted previously, fully-jacketed round-nosed bullets tend to over-penetrate. Therefore, in 1986 it was decided to make available to officers authorised to carry the Browning an alternative semi-wadcutter semi-jacketed round, that is, one with a flattened nose which is unsleeved and is therefore less likely to over-penetrate. Unfortunately, its shape means that it is rather less likely to travel easily up the ramp and into the breech. As a result the occurrence of jamming has increased since this ammunition has been in use.

Another important difference between the two types of weapon is that whereas revolvers can be fired in single or double-action, a self-loading pistol is fired only in the single-action mode. The mechanism of the self-loading pistol is operated by the recoil from the previously fired round, not by the depression of the trigger. Thus, each time a round is fired the mechanism pushes the hammer into the single-action position where the lightest touch on the trigger (five pounds in the case of the Browning) causes the hammer to fall and the round in the breech to be fired, which, in turn, activates the mechanism and pushes the hammer into the single-action mode. It is because self-loading pistols are so delicately poised in single-action, that they are almost universally equipped with safety catches. Unlike the revolver the self-loading pistol is not inherently safe and, therefore, safety has to be added by means of an external locking mechanism which prevents the trigger being depressed and a round being fired unintentionally. However, once the safety catch is released in anticipation of opening fire there is a greater risk of an accidental discharge than there would be with a revolver.

Some self-loading pistols incorporate a double-action mechanism for the first round fired. When the weapon is loaded, like all self-loading pistols, the first round is placed into the breech by 'racking' the slide manually. A catch is then depressed which causes the hammer to fall, but the gun does not fire because the hammer is not allowed to make contact with the firing-pin. When the first round comes to be fired, the trigger is depressed and this causes the hammer to open and fall onto the firing-pin as in double-action (although, of course, there is no cylinder to rotate). This gives an extra margin of safety with respect to the first shot fired, but thereafter the recoil slide mechanism ensures that all subsequent rounds are fired single-action. This offers some advantages over pistols like the Browning which fire only in single-action. Yet, it seems strange that when single-action shooting with revolvers has been discontinued on grounds of safety there should be pressure from within the force and outside of it to adopt a type of weapon that only fires in single-action.

From what has been said it may be assumed that this complex weapon is relatively unpopular, but this is not so. On the contrary, although a few instructors voice reservations about its utility as a police weapon, most prefer to carry it when on operational duties. Apart from its firepower, the self-loading pistol fires more rapidly (because of the reduced trigger travel) and more accurately (because of the reduced trigger pressure). It is unlikely that a single armed officer, even a member of a 'Level I' team, would have been able to hit three opponents with five shots as rapidly as did the officer at the Plumstead Abattoir had he not been armed with a self-loading pistol. In addition, self-loading pistols are quicker than revolvers to reload, for all the user need do is remove the empty magazine, replace it with a full one and release the catch. This automatically pushes the first round into the breech and leaves the gun in single-action, ready to fire. However, the development of 'jet loaders' for revolvers has diminished this advantage to some extent. These devices carry six rounds in a cylinder which complements the revolver cylinder and a mechanism which allows all six rounds to be injected into their respective chambers simultaneously and rapidly. The self-loading pistol also has the advantage of being slim (because it does not have a bulky cylinder) and is, therefore, much more readily concealed than is a revolver. It was for this reason that the Walther PP was issued to officers on plain clothes duties before it was withdrawn. There is pressure from some plain clothes branches to have the Browning issued more widely because it too would be more easily concealed. Perhaps another, but undeclared, reason for the Browning's popularity is that because it is such a complex and difficult weapon to use, and is restricted to Force Firearms Unit and officers of the Heathrow Airport Security Section, the Browning has much greater prestige than the standard revolver.

Whilst the self-loading pistol may be appropriate for officers who are highly skilled in their use, such as 'Level I' teams, it would seem that the disadvantages of this kind of weapon outweigh the advantages for more general use. Even when this kind of weapon is issued to highly specialised officers, it would seem prudent (in view of the fact that officers should always be deployed in pairs) for the partner to be equipped with the more reliable revolver. Alternatively, the British police may follow their American colleagues in allowing armed officers to carry an additional 'back-up gun' in case the primary weapon fails to operate or its ammunition becomes exhausted.

Sub-machine Guns

Of all the weapons issued to the police that which has attracted most criticism is the Heckler and Koch MP5 and MP5K. When it was announced that twelve Heckler and Koch MP5Ks had been purchased in anticipation of the summit of Western leaders in 1984, the Labour opposition demanded that these weapons be withdrawn (Gould and Waldren 1986). A similar furore erupted when some officers at Heathrow Airport were issued with the Heckler and Koch MP5 in February 1986 following attacks by Palestinian terrorists at Rome and Vienna airports the previous December.

The issue is not whether terrorists pose a serious threat to diplomats, politicians and airports. The fact that they do present such a threat is evidenced by attacks such as the attempted assassination of Sholom Argov, the Israeli Ambassador, in 1983 and the grenade and machine gun attack at Rome and Vienna airports in December 1985, which resulted in two passengers being killed and 47 injured at Vienna and 13 killed and 76 injured at Rome. The fact that Heathrow is not immune to terrorist activity was vividly illustrated in 1986 when Hussein Himdawi attempted to plant a bomb on board an El Al airliner departing from Heathrow. Unfortunately, these are only the most recent of a series of similar attacks staged in different parts of the world over the past 20 years.

The issue is whether the overt deployment of officers carrying the Heckler and Koch MP5 is operationally effective. The appearance of this weapon at Heathrow Airport led to protests that sub-machine guns are inappropriate for use in crowded airport terminals and could endanger bystanders. Indeed, it is true that all automatic weapons have a tendency to 'ride' and the Heckler and Koch MP5 certainly does so, tending to move diagonally across the target from bottom left to top right. Thus, although automatic weapons are designed to fire each individual round accurately in the direction the gun is aimed, the effect of the firing mechanism is to spray a succession of rounds across an area.

There may be occasions when automatic fire by police would be appropriate, such as a terrorist attack in open country or if the police had to mount an assault upon terrorist airliner hijackers who had begun killing hostages. However, it is clearly inappropriate for automatic fire to be used in an airport terminal building thronged with people. It is for precisely this reason that the Heckler and Koch MP5s deployed at Heathrow have been adapted to fire only single shots: they are not sub-machine guns but carbines which officers are taught to fire from the shoulder, not the hip. As such the MP5 is extremely accurate, there being hardly any recoil, so that even an untrained person can hit the target repeatedly. In many respects it is a much easier weapon to fire than either the revolver or self-loading pistol.

The need for such a weapon at Heathrow is two-fold: as mentioned earlier, its magazine of 30 rounds affords sufficient firepower to engage terrorists in a prolonged gunfight. At Rome and Vienna the terrorists attacked the El Al check-in queues with Kalashnikov AK47 assault rifles with two magazines of 30 rounds each taped together so that once the first magazine was exhausted the second could be inserted by the simple expedient of inverting the magazine and pushing it home. This meant that within the space of a few seconds, the three terrorists at Vienna and the four at Rome each had the opportunity to fire 60 rounds at a rate of 600 rounds per minute. The total attack at Vienna, including a car chase and second gunfight with police, lasted just seven minutes and that at Rome lasted only 55 seconds (Edwards and Menzies 1986). Given that the police may need to confront that kind of firepower, it is not difficult to appreciate the need for a weapon like the Heckler and Koch MP5.

The second reason for requiring a carbine is that police may need to engage terrorists at relatively long distances. Terminal buildings provide large open areas affording little cover and the piers connecting the various gates for boarding aircraft are enormously long corridors again offering restricted cover. In addition, airports include large open areas where terrorists might attack airliners waiting to take off. The maximum effective range of the handgun is optimistically estimated at 50 metres. Rifles can fire accurately over much greater distances, but suffer from problems of over-penetration. A carbine firing a normal 9mm pistol round can provide the additional range needed should a gunfight occur under these circumstances.

Apart from the confusion over whether the Heckler and Koch MP5 is a sub-machine gun or a carbine, there have been two other objections to its adoption for use at Heathrow Airport. The first is made by Yardley (1986) who (a) claims that carrying such a weapon is a symbolic victory for the terrorists who have forced the British police to abandon their non-aggressive image, (b) argues that it will make the police officer a prime target for terrorists, (c) doubts whether the weapon is intended to be aimed and fired from the shoulder, and (d) argues that if this is the intention then a dedicated carbine should have been preferred. Considering the last two points first, the Heckler and Koch MP5 issued to the Heathrow Airport Security Section has been modified to fire only single-shot and officers are trained to fire only aimed shots (as opposed to 'sense of direction') from the shoulder.

Why not, then, use a dedicated carbine which would not be confused with a sub-machine gun and avoid all the negative connotations of the latter? It is argued (Yardley 1986) that such a weapon could fire a round more suitable to police needs. Yardley points out that the Heckler and Koch MP5 normally fires a 9 mm round-nosed fully-jacketed round, which,

as mentioned previously, tends to over-penetrate, lacks
'stopping power' thereby, and tends also to ricochet. However,
dedicated carbines are magazine fed weapons which also
normally fire round-nosed fully-jacketed rounds. Moreover, in
fact the Metropolitan Police now issue a semi-wadcutter semi-
jacketed round of less power than the military 2Z round to
which Yardley seems to be referring. This bullet does not
over-penetrate nor is it so likely to ricochet as the
military-style round, albeit that it is more prone to jam the
firing mechanism. Of course, these same rounds could be used
in a dedicated carbine with the same advantages and
disadvantages. An advantage in doing so might be that they
could not be confused with sub-machine guns, and thus not
convey such an aggressive militaristic image. However,
dedicated carbines such as the Stirling Mk7 C4 and C8 are
indistinguishable from sub-machine guns and would do as much
damage to the image of the police as the Heckler and Koch MP5.
It is doubtful whether other carbines which have the
appearance of rifles would be any more acceptable to public
opinion.

The second challenge is altogether more substantial and is
contained in a report on the Rome and Vienna terrorist attacks
written by Chief Superintendent Edwards and Detective Sergeant
Menzies of the Sussex Police, who are responsible for security
at Gatwick Airport (Edwards and Menzies, 1986). They visited
Rome and Vienna airports in the wake of the terrorist attacks
of 1985 to examine the implications of these attacks for
airport security at Gatwick. Their report points out that
despite the fact that at least some of the officers who
engaged the terrorists at both airports were armed with sub-
machine guns only one officer used this weapon and did so in
single-shot mode. The authors of this report remark that at
Vienna:

> It is significant that although armed with the Steyr sub-
> machine gun the officers chose the 9mm pistols as the
> more appropriate weapon for use inside the terminal.

At Rome:

> The majority of the rounds were fired from Beretta

pistols . . . The sniper overlooking the concourse could not fire because of the confusion below.

They conclude:

The use of machine guns by police in the terminal building is not recommended because of the numbers of passengers that could be reasonably expected.

and

Hand guns used by trained officers can compete effectively against sub-machine guns in close combat.

Advocates of the Heckler and Koch MP5 amongst Metropolitan Police firearms instructors reply to this argument by pointing out that it is often the practice on the Continent, where officers are permanently armed with handguns, to use the sub-machine gun as the 'back-up weapon' rather than the primary weapon. Officers at Heathrow armed with the Heckler and Koch MP5 are trained to regard this as their primary weapon and their handgun as their 'backup'. Hence the Heckler and Koch MP5 is carried in the 'high port' position which facilitates ease of use, being very rapidly aimed and fired from the shoulder. However, even if accepted, this does not refute the point that in actuality, the use of handguns *was* effective against terrorists armed with automatic rifles.

A further point to emerge from the Edwards and Menzies report was that at Rome and Vienna only those officers in the immediate vicinity of the attack were able to engage the terrorists. At Vienna, the report notes:

Of the number of police officers inside the terminal building only 2 were in a position to respond to the attack by using firearms, the remainder were thwarted by the number of passengers who were running away from the attack.

A similar situation occurred at Rome where only three of the ten or more officers on duty in the terminal were able to engage the attackers. Thus, the report concludes:

> Because of the number of passengers likely to be in the
> check-in area it is probable that a small number of
> officers will be able to respond to a terrorist attack.

Apart from pointing to the need to place available officers at
strategic locations, this also suggests that the extra range
afforded by the Heckler and Koch MP5 will not be needed. On
the other hand, an attack on a pier or gate area may require
officers to engage terrorists at some distance.

Whilst the Edwards and Menzies report challenges some aspects
of the decision to deploy officers carrying the Heckler and
Koch MP5 inside the terminals at Heathrow Airport, it *does*
recommend that automatic weapons be available for the area
outside the terminal.

Thus, there are conflicting and equally convincing arguments
for and against the deployment of the Heckler and Koch MP5 at
Heathrow Airport which preclude any simple conclusion being
arrived at. Given the potential threat of terrorist attack, it
seems only right that officers should be equipped with weapons
necessary to protect passengers and deter terrorists. On the
other hand, the sight of British police officers carrying what
appears to be a sub-machine gun obviously damages the unarmed
image of the force as a whole.

Incidentally, the Edwards and Menzies report (1986) undermines
one of the criticisms levelled by Yardley, who argues that:

> The irony is that high profile security is ineffective.
> At the most obvious level because walking around in
> uniform and carrying a sub-machine gun is akin to walking
> around with a target pinned to you. (1986, p 20)

However, at Rome and Vienna the police were not the targets of
the terrorists, who concentrated upon their attacks on the
check-in queues alone. At Vienna the terrorists ignored two
police officers standing at the top of the stairs from which
they launched their attack on the waiting passengers.

Yet it seems difficult to deny that issuing this weapon has damaged the image of the unarmed British police officer. Certainly, photographs of officers carrying this weapon seem frequently to adorn newspaper and magazine articles on the police, especially anything remotely to do with firearms. This poses as clearly as almost anything else, the dilemma that must be faced between technical effectiveness and the need to retain legitimacy as a non-threatening force.

Overt versus Covert Carrying of Guns

The need to balance effectiveness against wider considerations applies equally to the general question of whether police should carry handguns overtly, outside their clothing, or covertly. Not only do armed officers in plain clothes covertly carry firearms, so too do armed officers in uniform. This is quite unusual, if not unique, amongst police forces throughout the world. On the one hand, this prevents the public being alarmed by the sight of visibly armed police and avoids a distinction being drawn between armed and unarmed officers. On the other hand, it hampers an armed officer who might need to draw his gun from the holster hidden under his tunic, as it did when PC Trevor Lock was overpowered by terrorists attacking the Iranian Embassy before he could draw his gun. Officers in shirt sleeves have an even greater problem, for the only opportunity for carrying the gun covertly is in a holster inside the trouser pocket, which makes the gun extremely difficult to draw in an emergency. Officers in some forces are equipped with a special pouch covered by a flap secured by velcron, which can quickly be ripped open and the gun drawn. Even so, this is obviously a more difficult manoeuvre than simply drawing the gun from a holster worn openly on the hip.

There are also anomalies, especially at Heathrow Airport where members of the Security Section are permanently armed. First, amongst those officers in this section a distinction is drawn between those who overtly carry the Heckler and Koch MP5 and are, therefore, allowed also to carry their handgun overtly, and those who are simply armed with handguns which they must carry covertly. It is argued by some officers that since the Heckler and Koch MP5 is carried overtly any damage to the unarmed image of the British police has been already been inflicted. Also, the justification for carrying the Heckler and Koch MP5 is that a terrorist attack may occur suddenly, without warning and be of such brief duration that an officer may need immediately to return fire. The same surely applies to other officers of the Security Section, each of whom might be impeded in drawing their covertly carried handgun from the holster under the same circumstances. A second anomaly is that officers who carry guns covertly cannot be easily distinguished from unarmed officers engaged on 'general duties'. In the event of a terrorist attack, insofar as police might be the targets of the attackers, unarmed officers will be at as much risk as their armed colleagues. However, there is a compensating advantage that not knowing which police officers are or are not armed may cause terrorists to over-estimate the odds they might face in mounting an attack.

There seems little reason to doubt that the effectiveness of armed officers in combatting a terrorist attack would be enhanced if they wore their firearms overtly. The difficulty lies in weighing these quite tangible benefits against the damage that this would do to the image of the unarmed, non-aggressive British bobby. The response of the Home Office Working Party (1986a) to the suggestion that weapons should normally be carried overtly was hostile. They insisted that overtly carrying weapons, such as the Heckler and Koch MP5, is an exceptional measure in response to exceptional conditions.

Short Versus Long Barrelled Revolvers

An issue related to the overt versus covert carrying of weapons is the type of weapon that should be issued to officers in plain clothes who must, of necessity, carry a firearm covertly. It was for officers engaged on these duties that the Walther PP was originally intended, because it is a compact weapon. However, when that weapon was withdrawn in 1974 it was replaced by the short-barrelled, five chamber version of the standard model 10 Smith and Wesson, the model

36 (Scientific Advisory Branch 1972). In 1983 the model 36 was, in turn, replaced with the six chamber version of the same weapon, the model 64, which is of stainless steel construction.

The justification for choosing the models 36 and 64 is that their two-inch barrels make them easier to conceal and less cumbersome to carry routinely. However, the disadvantage of this weapon is that it is less accurate over long distances (Greenwood 1979 and Harold 1974). This is now officially acknowledged, since officers authorised to use the model 64 need only qualify in aimed shooting at a maximum of 15 metres compared to the 25 metre range of the model 10. The short distance between the foresight and backsight on the model 64 means that it is difficult to achieve accurate alignment and any small error at the point of aim is magnified with increased distance. Moreover, the stainless steel construction reflects light and often obscures the sight-picture, making this weapon particularly difficult to aim. On the other hand, it is thought that this weapon is unlikely to be used at long distances, for it is mainly issued to officers engaged on close protection duty where they may have to combat an attack at close quarters. However, the only occasion to date where a protection officer has been called upon to use a short-barrelled revolver - the attempted assassination of the Israeli Ambassador in 1983 - involved him shooting a carefully aimed shot at the escaping would-be assassin who was 15 metres away (*The Times* 6 April 1987).

The advantage of concealment over accuracy would be more convincing if the length of barrel was critical to concealing a revolver. Unfortunately, the most difficult features of any revolver to conceal are the cylinder and the butt, which, in the case of the model 64, are virtually identical to the model 10. It seems difficult to disagree with Greenwood (1979) or Harold (1974), who argues that the balance of advantage lies with the longer barrelled revolver, particularly since the 'pancake holster' makes even this bulky weapon easy to conceal. However, if concealment is of such overriding importance then it would seem that a self-loading pistol, similar to the Walther PP, is what is required.

The Selection of Weapons

The selection of weapons which are less than completely appropriate to the task is encouraged, in the view of some instructors, by the procedures through which any given weapon is adopted. Essentially, this is a consultative process in which a compromise must be reached between the technical merits of the firearm, as judged by PT17, and its 'user acceptability', as judged by the department or branch whose officers will carry the weapon. It is felt by many instructors that too much attention is given to the inexpert view of the 'users' and insufficient attention to the evaluation of the firearms experts who will be responsible for training officers in the weapon's use. It certainly seems ludicrous that a weapon, such as the model 64, should be officially issued when it is held in such obvious contempt by the acknowledged experts.

Personal Issue Weapons

Before leaving the question of the weapons issued to armed police, one final issue which needs examining is the personal issue of weapons to individual officers. Apart from a small number of officers - mostly firearms instructors - who are issued with their own personal weapon, officers take or are given what is available from the armoury or safe. Thus, an AFO called to an incident will simply pick up a weapon of the type for which he is authorised, and which he may not have handled previously.

The problem with this is that all weapons differ, for example, in the amount of pressure needed to fire them in double-action. Also each individual officer will have his own physical characteristics, for example, some people have larger hands than do others. Thus, an officer could find himself in an armed operation holding a particular weapon which he has never fired before and he finds uncomfortable to grip. Certainly, people with large hands find it difficult to fire a gun accurately without special grips being fitted to the butt. Since his or someone else's life may depend upon his use of that weapon, this is clearly an unsatisfactory state of affairs.

The obvious solution is for all authorised officers to be issued with their own weapons, to which they could fit suitable grips and with which they could practise and become familiar. The objections to this are first that of cost: 3,000 authorised officers each equipped with a gun costing around £150 would mean a capital expenditure of approximately £450,000. This may seem prohibitively expensive, but it compares quite favourably with the cost of public order equipment, vehicles and other items of capital equipment. The second objection is that in order for the officer to have ready access to his personal issue weapon he would need to convey it to a secure place (such as a police station) near to wherever he happened to be on duty at the time. There would be a risk of insecurity and possible allegations that police were covertly arming themselves to a much greater extent than they publicly acknowledged. However, neither of these objections seems to outweigh the advantages to be attained from personally issuing weapons, as indeed is the practice in the army. Permanently armed officers seem to have a particularly strong case for being issued with their own weapon with which they can become familiar and for which they, and they alone, can be held responsible.

A possible solution to the logistic difficulties of ensuring that personal issue weapons are available when needed would be to adopt fully the notion of 'armed response vehicles' as now deployed by a few forces. Not only would the weapons carried on board such a vehicle be those issued to the crew members, but such a vehicle would be able to attend an armed incident very quickly and establish an initial containment. Following the Hungerford massacre in August 1987, there was criticism that armed police were too slow arriving at the scene (Edwards 1988). The coroner rightly rejected that criticism on the grounds that it was the price we all had to pay for the maintenance of a largely unarmed police force. However, armed response vehicles could reduce the inevitable delay in responding to armed incidents.

Armed response vehicles would have other benefits. At present, when an armed incident is reported the first police officers likely to arrive at the scene will be unarmed. They must do whatever they can to protect members of the public and contain the gunman, but their effectiveness in doing so is likely to be hindered by their being unarmed. Moreover, these unarmed officers are highly vulnerable and may fall victim to a gunman as did PC Brereton during the Hungerford massacre in August 1987. When armed officers do eventually arrive, they may do so singly and have to form themselves into pairs at the scene. This may involve being paired with another officer whom they do not know, or have not worked with closely, or with whom they have not trained – an obviously unsatisfactory situation given the seriousness of the circumstances. An armed response vehicle, by contrast, is not only likely to arrive first, but would contain a pair of officers who work together regularly on ordinary police duties and train together as AFOs. They would be in a position to establish an effective containment from the outset.

The police and the Home Office have been reluctant to endorse the deployment of armed response vehicles for reasons which appear less than convincing. The Home Office Working Party (1986a) saw no reason 'to commend the practice to chief officers', apparently on the grounds that such vehicles require that crews be trained both as drivers and AFOs. However, this is hardly a compelling objection since dog handlers have long been trained to drive emergency vehicles as an additional skill and there seems no reason why AFOs should not similarly be trained. What may concern policy-makers is the damage that such a deployment may inflict upon the traditional unarmed image of the British police and the controversy that such a move might occasion. However, in the wake of the Hungerford massacre and other recent highly publicised armed incidents, it is now likely that the public would accept this kind of deployment as necessary. If so, the newly-formed Territorial Support Groups, which maintain an immediate response capability in London, would seem the most appropriate unit to fulfil this function, since not only could they provide sufficient AFOs, but also additional officers to perform the tasks of the perimeter cordon.

A less radical alternative would be to allow officers to fit their own grips to any gun with which they were issued (Yardley and Eliot 1986c). The practical problem here is one of time, for this would delay officers drawing weapons from the armoury in an emergency. However, most firearms are not issued in emergency conditions and the time taken to fit grips is irrelevant. In the event of firearms being issued in an emergency the need for speed would obviously override the advantages of fitting personal grips. Either way, it is essential that additional resources should be found for the provision of this equipment.

Conclusions - Drifting Towards an Armed Police?

This chapter has considered whether the police have acquired a more deadly armoury than they strictly need. What has emerged is the genuine dilemma between ensuring immediate and effective incapacitation of a dangerous suspect and causing no more injury than is necessary. Superficially attractive suggestions, such as 'shooting to wound', turn out, upon examination, to pose greater risks to all concerned, instead of reducing them. The choice of ammunition which retains fidelity to the Hague Conventions may reduce the ability to incapacitate and pose a risk to innocent bystanders from over-penetrating and ricocheting bullets. The desire not to alarm the public by the sight of police overtly carrying firearms is achieved at a possible cost of preventing an officer from rapidly drawing his weapon. These are genuine, and perhaps inescapable, dilemmas which critics of the police seem reluctant to face.

Perhaps the greatest dilemma of all is whether in responding to armed crime and terrorism the British police are drifting gradually, but inexorably, towards becoming routinely armed, as are virtually all their counterparts throughout the world. The danger is not only that as crime and terrorism pose an increased threat the police will be drawn towards ever more frequent deployment of armed officers, but that it is more difficult to reverse direction once an escalatory step has been taken. An example of this kind of 'ratchet effect' can be seen at Heathrow Airport where the Heckler and Koch MP5 was deployed in response to the attack on Rome and Vienna airports. Despite the fact that authority for carrying these weapons must be obtained each month by the Home Office, and the firm wish amongst senior officers of the Metropolitan Police to remove these weapons once it is safe to do so, is unlikely that they will be withdrawn in the foreseeable future. If these weapons were to be withdrawn and this decision was to be followed by a terrorist attack at the airport it seems reasonable to suppose that the public outcry would be enormous. The police and the Home Office would be condemned for failing adequately to protect the public. Only the clearest indication that the risk to airports has been significantly reduced, if not eliminated, will encourage those in authority to take such a decision. However, it is in the nature of terrorist activity that it does not easily permit such a conclusion to be drawn. It is difficult to identify a point at which tension has lessened sufficiently to warrant a degree of disarmament. Whereas a particularly horrendous incident can *precipitate* an escalation towards armed policing, few comparable events can prompt a compensating de-escalation.

CHAPTER SEVEN

A TASK FOR THE POLICE?

For most of their history, it has been a matter of considerable pride that the British police perform their duties unarmed. As we have noted, this has never been strictly the case, but the image of the unarmed 'Bobby' has been one upon which the British police have founded their reputation and legitimacy in the eyes of other citizens. Accordingly, the sight of armed officers and incidents in which armed police confront armed criminals and terrorists, possibly exchanging shots, arouse a sense of public unease. In the climate of partisan politics which has surrounded policing in recent years, the image of the armed police officer can be, and has been, used to undermine the traditional legitimacy of the police. For the police officer there is the potential confusion between being the amiable 'community copper' one day and a gunman the next. In the words of one of the riflemen who appeared on the BBC TV programme, *The Queen's Peace:*

> We can't pat kids on the head one day and then shoot them with plastic bullets the next. (*Police* 1986)

A Third Force?

Faced with this (the most fundamental) dilemma, it is tempting to seek a solution which returns the police to their traditional role and allocates duties involving the use of firearms to some other paramilitary organisation. On the one hand, such a proposal is a retreat from reality, for there would never be sufficient paramilitary police available to deal with every armed incident. At a practical level this proposal merely translates to national proportions the difficulties of providing specialist squads of armed officers even in centres of population. As explained above, this is an expensive and ineffective option. It is also a retreat from the reality of what the police are: monopolists of force in civil society. The use of potentially lethal weapons is just the ultimate expression of that role, not a distraction from it.

On the other hand, there are armed tasks currently undertaken by the police which might merit separation from the generality of police work. The police, particularly the Metropolitan Police, have always performed various guarding duties: there have always been police bodyguards and they have usually been armed. The growth of international terrorism has caused this function to be extended massively. Airports throughout the United Kingdom are protected by armed police; the Royalty and Diplomatic Protection Department guards persons and places at risk from terrorist attack; beyond the civil police the Atomic Energy Authority Police (see *Time Out* 22 Oct 1986) and Ministry of Defence police both provide armed protection for sensitive installations. Whether performed by members of the civil police or not, the tasks they perform are essentially the same and distinguish them from the remainder of the police service. This is partially recognised in the case of the RDPD, whose vehicles have a distinctive maroon livery. All these departments of the Metropolitan Police or separate police forces perform a quasi-military, rather than police, role of providing protection from external attack. As already mentioned, it makes little sense to imagine police 'containing' a terrorist attack upon an airport terminal: the task of armed officers must be to engage and defeat.

Perhaps it is time that government considered establishing a national paramilitary security force to perform these guarding duties. If they wore a uniform which distinguished them from the police, they would be free to carry weapons overtly without undermining the traditional image of the unarmed British police. Directly responsible to government, the cost of such a corps would not be obscured by its inclusion with other police functions and inevitable competition for resources within the police budget. In areas like airport terminals, the separation of function would avoid anomalies and confusion, leaving the police to deal with routine policing tasks whilst the security force simply guarded against terrorist attack.

Even if this strategy were adopted, it would not eliminate the need for some police to use firearms some of the time. So long as this is a regrettable necessity, the police must commit themselves to maintaining and enhancing the professional approach that has been increasingly evident since the mid-1960s.

CHAPTER EIGHT

CONCLUSIONS

Clearly, the use of firearms by the police remains highly
controversial. The shooting of anyone, even in the most
apparently justified circumstances, invariably prompts lengthy
news reports and 'in-depth' analyses by the news media. The
civil liberties lobby are vocal in their criticism of police
use of firearms in general. Irritating though this scrutiny
and criticism might be for the police officers upon whom this
attention is focused, it should nevertheless be welcomed as a
sign of democratic health. If the police were able to shoot
suspects with impunity there would be no external check upon
their possibly over-zealous enforcement of the law. The dictum
that the price of liberty is eternal vigilance applies as
much, if not more so, to the police use of force as to any
other aspect of public life.

However, if scrutiny is to be effective and criticism well-
founded it is essential that commentators are well-informed.
It is clear that this has not always been the case with regard
to police use of firearms. In part this is undoubtedly due to
the enforced ignorance in which those outside the police have
been kept. Unfortunately, uninformed criticism often gives the
impression that it is motivated not only by ignorance but also
by malice. This then serves only to strengthen the resolve of
the police to restrict the availability of information lest
malicious critics misuse it. Hence, a vicious spiral of mutual
mistrust is created and becomes self-sustaining.

This report has sought to break this spiral and raise the veil
of secrecy surrounding this subject, in the hope that this
will stimulate an informed and productive debate. In doing so,
some of the wilder allegations of critics have been refuted

and some genuine misunderstandings corrected. This does not
mean that there are no causes for genuine concern nor
criticisms that can be levelled against the police. Several
issues merit continued discussion.

a) Despite considerable and welcome advances in the
training of AFOs, it remains the case that insufficient
attention is given to adequate *tactical* training. During
initial training officers have the opportunity only to
discover how likely it is that things will go wrong,
rather than how they should do the task properly.
Hopefully, they learn to approach actual incidents with
a degree of caution, but it seems hardly fair to allow
such minimally trained officers to assume the
potentially awesome responsibility of dealing with an
armed incident. At least, it would seem appropriate for
recently authorised AFOs to spend a period on probation
in much the same way as recently recruited constables
do. Steps could be taken to ensure that whenever
possible a probationary AFO was paired with an
experienced officer on armed operations.

b) Connected to the above is the issue of refresher
training and re-authorisation. The current requirement
to spend one day four times per year on refresher
training combined with a re-authorisation test is
plainly inadequate to maintain necessary standards of
competence. The plan to double the time spent on
refresher training to four two-day sessions per year
would seem to be the bare minimum and it is regrettable
that limited resources have meant that its introduction
will have to be staged over a number of years. In view
of the potential danger inherent in the operational use
of firearms, it is essential that sufficient resources
be made available to provide all AFOs with adequate
training, especially tactical training.

c) An even more urgent need is adequately to train incident
commanders so that they are fully aware of what the
various levels of armed officers can and cannot safely
do, and what tactical options are available to them. In
the field of public order policing the Metropolitan
Police have formed cadres of senior officers on each of
the force's eight Areas to take command of incidents.
Given the frequency of armed operations occurring in

London, there would seem to an even greater need for similar cadres of senior officers trained and able to command in these situations. What does seem difficult to justify is that the onerous burden of acting as a tactical adviser should rest on the junior shoulders of some unfortunate AFO.

d) Related to the previous point, it needs to be recognised that the proper handling of an armed incident relies on coordinated team work and not upon individuals acting separately. Hence, incident commanders must '*command*' and subordinates must act in accordance with those commands. However, it is only right that when subordinates follow orders, those who issue them should take some responsibility. The exclusive legal liability which now rests upon the officer holding the gun (who will not be the incident commander in the vast majority of cases) is incompatible with the need for coordinated team work. Of course, officers of all ranks must accept legal liability for their individual actions, but so too should those who command them.

e) It seems ludicrous that firearms instructors should hold an officially issued gun, the Smith and Wesson model 64, in such obvious contempt. If the weapon is regarded as so unsuitable by those whom the force regards as its experts, then it should not be issued at all. Whilst consultation and 'user evaluation' will continue to be necessary, there seems a strong case for allowing PT17 to exercise the greatest influence over the choice of weapons.

f) If the model 64 is an unsuitable weapon, so too is the Browning self-loading pistol for all but a few highly specialised officers. This is not only a highly complex piece of machinery, it fires only in single-action, a mode of shooting no longer permitted with revolvers. If a self-loading pistol is felt to be necessary for certain specialised functions, then it would seem only consistent to choose one which fires the first shot, at least, double-action. Given the susceptibility of these weapons to jamming, it would seem prudent to insist that an officer equipped with such a weapon should have a partner equipped with the more reliable revolver.

g) The demand for the greater firepower of self-loading pistols might be reduced if the ammunition issued to officers had greater stopping power. To require officers to rely on hitting the target with each of a pair of shots in order totally to incapacitate an opponent seems excessively demanding. Since existing ammunition breaches the Hague Conventions - Conventions which, in any case, do not and never have applied to policing - there seems no sound reason for refusing to issue ammunition, such as the .357" Magnum hollow-point, which will ensure that each shot will effectively incapacitate. This ammunition will, if fired, almost certainly prove fatal, but officers are not permitted to use firearms except in conditions which would justify them in killing a person. If they do fire a pair of shots, both of which hit the person, then the effect will probably be fatal anyway, so the use of more powerful ammunition will not, in practice, amount to a departure from the doctrine of minimum force.

h) What is urgently required is some alternative to the ball ammunition now supplied to riflemen, for this poses a genuine danger to innocent members of the public should it ever be used. It may be technically impossible to produce a high-velocity bullet which does not over-penetrate, but a soft-nose bullet would be much less likely to ricochet or penetrate walls and similar structures.

i) There is also a need for all AFOs, but particularly permanently armed officers such as those engaged in diplomatic protection, to be issued with their own individual gun. It seems strange that individual officers are equipped with their own personal riot equipment, but that others who might be asked to take life and death decisions should be expected to do so with a weapon with which they may well be unfamiliar - or, indeed, so uncomfortable that it is difficult to fire accurately. The difficulties of having personal issue weapons readily available in case of need could be overcome if the force adopted the policy of having 'armed response vehicles' - ordinary patrol cars which carry firearms in a locked safe which can only be opened with the authority of the appropriate senior officer.

This would ensure that not only would the crews of these vehicles have their personal issue weapons available, but also that they would be able to attend any armed incident and establish a containment speedily.

If public discussion about police use of firearms is to be well-informed, not only is it essential that these foregoing issues be considered, but also that some of the genuine dilemmas should be appreciated. There are some questions to which there are no simple answers. For example, there is a convincing case to be made for both the deployment and non-deployment of the Heckler and Koch MP5 at Heathrow Airport. Those who, in good faith, disagree with its deployment should not assume that those who come to the opposite conclusion do so out of malice or stupidity. What is clear is that this decision was taken with regret after considerable deliberation.

The most acute dilemma is not that faced by policy-makers, but that faced by their subordinates who must decide whether or not to draw their weapon from the holster, or to take aim, or to open fire. Sometimes an officer will have only a split-second in which to decide whether or not to fire his gun. If he makes the wrong decision, one way or the other, he may kill someone unnecessarily or be killed himself or allow some other innocent person to be killed. Given the conditions under which this decision must often be made, it is inevitable that mistakes will occur and other names will be added to those of Gail Kinchen and John Shorthouse, Stephen Waldorf and Cherry Groce, just as more officers will join Brian Bishop on the roll of honour and PC Sliman and Inspectors Beeton and Atkinson on the injured list (not to mention the list of unarmed officers who have been murdered on duty by gunmen). To their credit, the courts have insisted that when interpreting section 3 of the Criminal Law Act 1967 the test of 'reasonable force' should not be that of quiet contemplation, but what would appear reasonable to a person in the actual circumstances in which the decision had to be made. Unfortunately, others who judge police actions sometimes give the impression that they expect officers to display nothing short of exceptional courage and superhuman powers of deduction.

Has the correct balance been struck? Are the police armed sufficiently to cope with all but the most exceptional circumstances they are likely to face, whilst avoiding recourse to excessive force? These are questions which do not permit simple or definitive answers. The uncomfortable truth is that the use of force, especially deadly force, poses a number of dilemmas. There is a continual need to balance operational effectiveness against public acceptability in conditions which are changing and which, in turn, affect what is or is not publicly acceptable. It is, therefore, unlikely that the police will *ever* completely 'get it right'. Once these dilemmas are recognised, informed public debate about these issues can commence.

REFERENCES

Ayoob, M. (1984) *Stressfire*, M. and D. Ayoob, available from Police Bookshelf, Concord, New Hampshire

Benn, M. and Worpole, K. (1986) *Death in the City*, Canary Press, London

Bittner, E. (1970) *The Functions of the Police in a Modern Society*, US Govt Printing Office, Washington DC

Bittner, E. (1974) Florence Nightingale in pursuit of Willie Sutton: A theory of the police, in Jacob, H. (ed.), *The Potential for Reform in Criminal Justice*, Sage, Beverly Hills

Critchley, T.A. (1970) *The Conquest of Violence*, Constable, London

Critchley, T.A. (1978) *A History of Police in England and Wales*, Constable, London

Edwards, C. (1988) Was Hungerford "a basic failure of the police"? *The Listener*, 14 January, pp 4-5.

Edwards, G.S. and Menzies, K. (1986) *Visits to Leonardo Da Vinci Airport, Rome, and Schwechat Airport, Vienna*, Sussex Police unpublished report, Gatwick Airport

Emsley, C. (1983) *Policing and its Context*, Macmillan, London

Gould, R.W. and Waldren, M.J. (1986) *London's Armed Police*, Arms and Armour, London

Greater London Council (1984) *Proposed inquiry into the issuance and use of firearms by police in London*, London

Greenwood, C. (1966)   *Police   Firearms   Training*,   Forensic
Science Society, London

Greenwood, C. (1979)   *Police Tactics   in   Armed   Operations*,
Paladin Press, Boulder, Colorado

Greenwood, C. (1986) Where gun training fails, *Police Review*,
10 October, pp 2065-66

Harold, M.C.D. (1974) Armaments for police officers on
protection, *Police Jnl*, 47, October, 293-300

Hoare, M. (1980) *The Pattern of Experience in the use of
Firearms by Criminals and the Police Response*, unpublished MSc
thesis, Cranfield Institute of Technology

Home Office (1983) *Guidelines for the Police on the Issue and
Use of Firearms*, circular 47/1983, London

Home Office (1986a) *Report by the Home Office Working Group on
the Police Use of Firearms*, London

Home Office (1986b) *Criminal Statistics England and Wales
1985*, Cm 10, HMSO, London

International   Law   Enforcement,   (1985a) Police   firearms
training in the United Kingdom, part I, 1, no 5, 20-23

International   Law   Enforcement,   (1985b) Police   firearms
training in the United Kingdom, part II, 1, no 6, 17-20

Jacobs, J. and Sanders, A. (1986) Should police be armed? *New
Society*, 11 July, pp 12-13

Manolias, M. and Hyatt-Williams, A. (1988) *Post-Shooting
Experiences in Firearms Officers*, SRDB-ACPO Joint Working
Party on Organisational Health and Welfare, Home Office,London

Manwaring-White, S. (1983) *The Policing Revolution*, Harvester,
Brighton

Miller, W.R. (1977) *Cops and Bobbies: Police Authority in New York and London, 1830-1870,* University of Chicago Press, Chicago

Milton, C.H., Halleck, J.W., Lardner, J. and Abrecht, G.L. (1977) *Police Use of Deadly Force,* Police Foundation, Washington

Police, (1983) Guns: Whitelaw tells police: "You're on your own", May, p 20

Police, (1986) Community bobbies one day - trained to kill the next, November, pp 8-9

Punch, M. (1979) *Policing the Inner City,* Macmillan, London

Rae, A. (1987) The medals of the Met, *Police Review,* 30 January, pp 226-7

Reiner, R. (1985) *Politics of the Police,* Wheatsheaf, Brighton

Roberts, B.R. (1973) Arms for the police, *Police College Magazine,* 12, 4, pp 19-23

Rubinstein, J. (1973) *City Police,* Farrar, Strauss and Giroux, New York

Rusbridger, J. (1985) Letter to *Daily Telegraph,* 17 September

Scientific Advisory Branch (1972) *Firearms for Police Use in Peacetime,* Home Office, London

Stead, P.J. (1985) *The police of Britain,* Macmillan, London

Waddington, P.A.J. (1986) Letter to *New Society,* 25 July

Waddington, P.A.J. (1988) The unacceptable price of a routinely armed police force, *The Independent,* 7 January, p 16

Yardley, M. (1986) Wrong, *Police,* XVIII, February , 20-21

Yardley, M. and Eliot, P. (1986a) Is police firearms training good enough? *Police*, XVIII, May, 14-16

Yardley, M. and Eliot, P. (1986b) The case for special units *Police*, XVIII, June, 26-31

Yardley, M. and Eliot, P. (1986c) Wanted: a national firearms school, *Police*, XVIII, July, 20-21